Fishing for Fun

FISHING
FOR FUN

Byron Dalrymple

Winchester Press

The chapters in this book appeared originally, in some cases under slightly different titles, in various periodicals, as follows: "The Wondrous Ways of Fishermen," *Sports Afield,* April 1960, © 1960 by The Hearst Corp.; "Never Catch a Muskie!," *True's Fishing Yearbook* No. 21, © 1970 by Fawcett Publications, Inc.; "Blue Runners: Dynamite on Light Tackle," *Sports Afield,* March 1956, © 1956 by The Hearst Corp.; "How to Find and Catch Trophy Bass," *Field & Stream,* January 1972, © 1972 by Field & Stream Magazine; "Tennessee Tarpon: The Skipjack Herring," *Sports Afield Fishing Annual,* 1956, © 1956 by The Hearst Corp.; "The Fish That Aren't Afraid," *Sports Afield,* May 1960, © 1960 by The Hearst Corp.; "The Dolly Varden: Who Says They're Trash Trout?," *True's Fishing & Hunting Yearbook* No. 15, © 1964 by Fawcett Publications, Inc.; "How to Be Happy with Walleyes," *True's Fishing Yearbook* No. 18, © 1967 by Fawcett Publications, Inc.; "Smallmouth Bass Are Different," *Outdoor Life,* June 1962, © 1962 by Popular Science Pub. Co., Inc.; "How Big a Pan Have You Got?," *True's Fishing Yearbook* No. 18, © 1967 by Fawcett Publications, Inc.; "Mining Bass in Kansas," *True's Fishing Yearbook* No.16, © 1965 by Fawcett Publications, Inc.; "A Plug for Trout Plugging," *Field & Stream,* June 1952, © 1952 by Field & Stream Magazine; "The Yellow Bass: The Fish Nobody Knows," *Sports Afield Fishing Annual,* 1957, © 1957 by The Hearst Corp.; "Primer for the New Pike Fisherman," *Outdoor Life,* June 1973, © 1973 by Popular Science Pub. Co., Inc.; "Sharp as a Cutlass," *Sports Afield,* December 1960, © 1960 by the Hearst Corp.; "How to Seduce a Fish," *True,* July 1969, © 1969 by Fawcett Publications, Inc.; "Catching Trout in the West," *Field & Stream,* June 1968, © 1968 by Field & Stream Magazine; "The Paddlefish: Mystery Monster from Missouri," *True's Fishing & Hunting Yearbook* No. 15, © 1964 by Fawcett Publications, Inc.; "The Most Diminutive Salmon," *Sports Afield,* May 1967, © 1967 by the Hearst Corp.; "You Don't Need to Carry a Cookbook," *True's Fishing Yearbook* No. 19, © 1968 by Fawcett Publications, Inc.

Library of Congress Catalog Card Number: 74-16870
ISBN: 0-87691-164-5

Published by Winchester Press
460 Park Avenue, New York 10022

Printed in the United States of America

TO THE EDITORS, past and present, of the magazines where these stories first appeared. Writing for them over the years has been almost as enjoyable as the fishing—and besides, it made the fishing possible!

Contents

CONTENTS

Introduction

For over five decades I've pursued the hobby of fishing, and for more than three I've been writing about it. Unless one is an accountant type, which I am not, a fishing career of that kind does not start with careful planning at Point A and progress with precision of learning step by step to Point B. Instead, it is a most pleasant kind of unplanned, helter-skelter gathering of experiences that, one sees eventually, somehow miraculously have a loose coherence, fitting together if one takes time to fit them, like a jigsaw puzzle, or just lying loose in the box.

This book is much the same. Life today it seems to me is already too mathematical, regimented, and systematized. Thus, I do not ask that you start this book at page 1 and read until you bump into the back cover. Shake the pieces up in the box and put them together, if you feel like it, later. Start with the final chapter, or the first, the middle, or any in between. Let your purpose hang loose, too, reading at any given moment to ferret out how-to facts, or simply—I hope—for enjoyment.

That's how it was, I understand now on looking back. I seized any fishing opportunity at any given moment just because it was there, sometimes to learn, studying hard, often just for relaxation or to add a new and brightly different experience. These chapters, pulled somewhat randomly from the card file of memory in the form of earlier writings, will I hope share a scattering of what I learned and experienced, in roughly the same hodge-podge manner in which I rather unwittingly absorbed both learning and experience as the years moved along.

Long ago I came to understand, I believe, the varied motivations of individual anglers. Some are species-dedicated, wanting desperately perhaps to collect a trophy largemouth bass, or to dope out the perplexing personality of the smallmouth. The muskie wholly mesmerizes but wildly exasperates others until in desperation they'll try anything, just in case. Walleye addicts can't quit, but often wistfully wish they could magically make their favorite a better battler. Eastern trout fishermen long to trek West, where it's "really at," and some go only to discover to their chagrin that East is East and West is far, far different. They're sad and empty in the creel.

Therefore some solid "how-to" from what the years have taught me is here to help you solve those and other problems. But there are certain anglers who are endlessly overwhelmed and intrigued by the new and unusual fishing experience. They're dedicated to catching varieties they've not caught previously, even though in the rather arrogant caste system we arbitrarily assign to our native fishes these may be represented as totally inconsequential. These overlooked or scorned opportunities have always drawn me like a magnet, and so some of these also are included. So are some of the ingenious, and kooky, schemes that anglers—myself included—have concocted to seduce fish, a facet of fishing that for me has been a lifetime fixation.

So that's what this book is. Let me also tell you what it *isn't*. There are no narratives of faraway places where only the few will ever find adventure. Rather, it's about places anyone can go, knowledge anyone can put to good use, experiences anyone can have. Nor is it a brag about all the big ones the author has caught. There've been a few, but they never came easily, or in batches. Perhaps, however, it may help you find your few—and if not, and far more important, at least lead you to additional fishing enjoyment.

1
The Wondrous
Ways of Fishermen

It was dark and the single light on the old broken-down saltwater boat dock laid a yellow pool of light upon the still Florida bay water. Below, working over some fish cleanings that lay on the bottom, thousands of small glut herring swirled with dizzying endless circling. They were almost a solid mass and they were blindingly swift, their silver bellies flashing like uncounted Fourth of July pinwheels.

I was casting for whatever might hit. I was catching nothing. I knew these tiny herring were excellent bait, and I wished I had one to try. But how to catch it?

Presently a well-weathered old native came padding down the pier. He carried a bait bucket. When he drew near, he looked sharply below the light and grunted approval. "Got to catch me a bait or two," he said.

He now produced a wondrously ingenious device. He had started with a 3-foot strand of light wire leader, had brought the two ends together and twisted them securely. Then he had flattened the circle, and, using what now were two strands joined at top and bottom, he had at brief intervals twisted them to make a continuous chain of figure-8s. To one end he had tied a length of ordinary black casting line. I could not imagine at first what he was up to.

But now he dangled the contraption down among the swirling mass of glut herring. This small fish, if laid on its side, would make almost a diamond-shaped pattern, so deep is it in the center of its body. Yet it is very compressed, and the keel is exceedingly sharp. It suddenly dawned on me that the wise old bird had made the loops of his figure-8s just a wee bit smaller than the depth of the average baitfish.

There was a sudden minor jerk and the line he held in his hand zipped off at an angle. He lifted quickly. There, stuck in the loops of his wire, were three glut herring, wriggling frantically but unable to free themselves. He popped them into his bait bucket. He grinned at my astonishment.

He said, "So many of 'em down there, they zip right into the loops. They can't swim backwards so they struggle forward and stick all the tighter." He proceeded to fill his bait bucket in a short time and padded back up to the dock. I sat there wondering. Where did the idea originate? Who dreamed it up, and how? I've never heard of it since.

In many years of fishing I have met thousands of fishermen. The ones who cling most sharply in memory are not the purists, the public-eye figures, the record-breakers, the expert casters. Rather, they are the few super-ingenious unsung souls like this one with the twisted wire. They are the ones who somehow, somewhere, through a bright flash of insight have fallen upon some small but unique and immensely useful idea.

The world of fishing is awash with these obscure methods and gimmicks. Trouble is, their very obscurity blocks attempts to gather them into one place of easy reference. Hunting them down is an exacting, useful hobby. In my opinion, some of the most valuable fishing lore is thus hidden away.

Remember that the old country geezer who began fishing as a boy did not necessarily always fish for sport. To him, over the years, fishing may have been at times exceedingly important because the need for the catch was serious. And so perhaps he came—maybe even in desperation—to invent ways and means. Or by happy circumstance he stumbled upon some little thing that made the big difference.

When I was a boy the cisco was a most important commercial species in the Great Lakes region. At times when these fish swarmed near shore, country fishermen would slip a small white button over the barb of a hook, and, using a long cane pole and line, sweep this oddity, held down with a small stovebolt nut for a sinker, back and forth, back and forth. What the ciscoes thought the button was, I don't know. But they'd bite the hook and get flopped out upon the shore. Who, I wonder, discovered this trick, and how. Today slick lures replace the button.

Or consider the sturgeon spearmen. There have been numerous stories over the years about the sport of spearing sturgeon through the ice in the Great Lakes region. But years ago this was not sport. It was a way of getting steaks for the table. All up through the north country one of the devices used to lure sturgeon near enough were bunches of yellow ears of corn dangled down into the hole. Why? Who cares! It worked. That was good enough. The intriguing part is—who discovered the attraction?

3

Left: In early days around the Great Lakes, ciscoes like these were caught by raking a white button on a hook through schools. Later on, modern flyfishermen learned to catch them on flies. *Right:* A huge sturgeon speared through the ice. Old-timers hung yellow ears of corn in the hole to attract the big fish.

In the wonderful world of baits, for example, there are endless bits of knowledge that have been "secrets" here and there maybe for centuries, yet to many of us today they are as new as next year's killer lure. After we have thought up every conceivable bait for every conceivable species of fish, along comes someone who learned from someone about a

4

"something" that has 'em all beat. This, again, takes me back to boyhood.

There was an old gentleman who lived not far from us who was known thereabouts as a "woodsie." This term was not used in a complimentary manner. It meant he was shiftless and just wanted to hunt and fish and prowl the woods while his scratch-dirt farm went, as they said, "to pot." Well, such a man was, in my boyhood estimation, smarter than the rest. He had seen the light, and followed it. And I, whenever I could sneak away, followed him.

One spring day I watched him sitting on the bank of a pond formed by a beaver dam on a small creek. Beside him were some of the most beautiful brook trout I had ever seen. Others caught trout in the pond, but not trout like these. With a boy's directness, not realizing what fabulous secrets I was prying into, I asked right out what he was using for bait.

"I had an uncle," he replied, "who made himself a million dollars. You know how? By minding his own business."

That shut me up. I sat and said nothing, and after a time I suppose maybe the old bird's heart was softened a mite. He put down his pole and began to stalk off into the woods. Then he turned.

"I'm out of bait," he said. "Want to help me get more?"

We prowled. My heart filled with delight, for I, too, would now have the secret. He studied a rotted log here, another there. One appeared just right to him. He got down on one knee and turned it over quickly. And just as quickly his hand shot forward. He extended it toward me, cupped tightly, then opened it only a crack. In his palm was a small lizardlike creature, a tiny newt or salamander.

There are millions of anglers to this day who would not know a newt if it carried a sign bearing its name and picketed them. But the so-called "spring salamander" (there are nu-

An old man showed me how to catch small salamanders, and what sensational bait they are.

merous varieties and they are found in many parts of the country in and beneath rotting logs in the woods) is one of the most devastating baits it is possible to use, for trout, for bass, for many kinds of fish. My old boyhood friend hooked one very gently through a leg and dropped it into the pond. He was fast to a big brookie before the bait had wriggled twice. Over the years I have known this odd bait to elicit striking results (no pun) many times when nothing else would.

But it is not always the grownups who make the discoveries and teach the kids. Youngsters often are the great innovators simply because they don't know what *won't* work. They have no set of rules already formed and so what won't work is what they try—and often as not, it does.

I was fishing a Western stream a couple of years ago and if it had trout in it I couldn't prove the point to anybody by exhibiting what was in my creel. I came about to the end of my run, and rounding a bend, there sat a boy on an old sideroad bridge. A homemade stringer dangled down into the water. On it was a goodly collection of trout of three species. The kid was using an old, cheaply made bamboo fly rod with frayed windings to which was attached a tarnished bait-casting reel filled with black casting line. No leader. Just a small sinker and a hook. And on the hook, as nearly as I could see, some variety of fat white grub.

He said, "Hullo," and rebaited from a tin can beside him. He dropped the bait down into the deep pool below the bridge.

I was fascinated. I stood watching, wondering where the heck he found fat white grubs this time of year. It was early spring and all but snowing. Presently he caught another trout. No stylish play. He grated the old reel as fast as it would go and got the fish in — so he could hurry up and get to catching another.

He turned to me and grinned. "Sure works good," he said.

Aha! Now I was going to learn the secret! "What works good?"

"Well," he said, hitching one leg up and spitting into the pool with great importance. "Ma had a bunch of leftovers this noon and I didn't like mine. Tough. And all I could think of, looking at it, was grubs. Then I think, 'Grubs!' Them things will do it! Look—"

He proffered the can. It was filled with short, fat, U-shaped pieces of cooked macaroni!

Now my point is this. It is not in the least important whether or not you ever bait trout with macaroni. But it is the melding of scores of such oddments that, becoming through years of experience a "whole," goes to make up the full-turned, canny, and truly successful angler. You may not actually *use* any of the bits and pieces you have gathered, as

7

such, and especially not the screwball ones. But meanwhile you will have learned always to be seeking such bits, grasping them, adding them to your personal store of knowledge. By such training in awareness, you come to know how to apply what is needed in every conceivable fishing situation.

I can recall vividly the first time I saw anyone fishing a worm *upstream* for trout. Not many anglers do it even today, yet it is brilliantly successful, and was the forerunner of proper artificial nymph fishing. I can remember precisely where and from whom I learned to catch an uncatchable brown trout by offering him exactly the opposite of what he was taking—a huge fly instead of a tiny one—and methodically casting it ten, twenty, fifty, a hundred times if necessary, until at last out of annoyance or curiosity he batted it. I thought the fisherman was crazy. He was—like a fox!

I remember two different fishermen, one after trout up

Giant flies as big as small bats often catch big brown trout at night.

8

North, one after bass down South, neither of them having any luck until their personal lightning struck. In each case the fish were taking large live insects flying just above the water. No floating fly could turn the trick. But a real live specimen stuck with chewing gum to a hook with a bit of cork on it to float it buzzed along and murderously did the required job.

Knacks, kinks, gimmicks—call them what you will. The sum of them is a fish-catching whirlwind of a fisherman. How does the finished angler know that he has only to take away from a blasé fish the bait or lure it spurns—to take it away in lifelike little jerks and pauses—and thus immediately awaken interest? Yet, this is fundamentally only a kind of horizontal jigging. And see how it can be applied in endless ways.

For example, I was fishing one spring with my two boys on a Texas Gulf Coast pier, for small spadefish. These fish are all but uncatchable—unless you know how. A tiny hook, a tiny bait, a hand quicker than the nip of the fish. None of us could get the hang of it. I would let my bait down, having found exactly the proper sinker weight, and then I would bring it up—jig, jig, jig, a little at a time. I observed that I could thus bring up with it a whole covey of the broad-striped disc-shaped spades. But they wouldn't strike. They'd just follow.

Suddenly I was, in memory, 2,000 miles away and it was bitter winter. Ice below me was a foot thick. I was on a bay of Lake Huron, fishing for yellow perch with what was then called a "Russian hook." This most intriguing lure is a metal spoon, wide at the top, narrow at the bottom, with hook brazed to the inner curved surface. It flutters enticingly when let down and jigged upward with short strokes. The trick is to flutter it upward, mesmerizing the perch into following. Then you suddenly drop it back a couple of inches, inert and twirling downward. *Whammo!* Instantly at the

9

strike you renew the upward motion and sweep the foolish perch right out atop the ice.

And so with the spadefish. I brought them up. I suddenly let the bait drop back, fluttering. Instantly one hit. Aha! I had him. I showed my two boys how. It took them a good many tries, but after a while they got it. Here indeed was a lesson in applying odd bits of angling knowledge. The base of usefulness was broad as the ends of the earth.

Nor is that the end of it. In past years I watched numerous times how Carl Allen, an old Michigan buddy of mine with many more years of experience than I, would work a bait-and-spinner combo while trolling or casting for bass, trout, bluegills—anything. Tap, tap, tap the strike would come. I'd jerk away, trying to stick the hook home. Carl would grin and do exactly the opposite.

Instead of reeling or striking, he'd let his bait drop back. No gentle, teasing forward motion, like the "experts" say. Nope. He'd kill it. And then, without feeling any bite at all because of course his line was slack, he'd pull smartly in a long, hard yank—and have his fish. He knew all too well that a fish following a lure and not hitting in a businesslike manner will, when the lure suddenly falls back limply, lunge and seize it, no longer curious but now out to kill and swallow an injured, helpless thing. Again, a skillful application of the ancient jigging art.

All such oddments plucked from specific places and times seem at first glance unrelated. But this very disrelation serves to illustrate what a wondrous accumulation of knowledge there must still be, lying around unaccumulated. Field-won knowledge, gleaned by endless hours of thinking, of observing, of fishing, of scheming how to outwit the seemingly non-outwittable. What a shame we cannot somehow unearth it all!

Especially curious to me is the fact that so much of this

scattered lore is really brilliant, yet has come, so often, from sources that seem quite the opposite.

Once I fished beside a very odd old gent at a little village on the California coast. Where we were operating there was a jumble of rock lying in great tumbled masses both above and beneath the surface. Among these rocks, as in many places along the Pacific, live thousands of rockfishes and sea basses of endless variety. Let a bait down and almost instantly something will have it. But you will not have the fish hooked for long. It darts back into a crevice and you cannot get it out. It breaks you off and that is that. Fishing here, I soon came to learn, was utterly senseless. That was before I saw this man.

He was shabbily dressed and shuffling. On his back he wore a homemade leather case that looked a bit like an archer's quiver. In it were numerous steel (or welding-rod) shafts several feet long. They differed in thickness. Many were possibly $3/16$-inch. Soldered to the tip of each was a ring in which to fasten a hook, and on the other end a place to tie the line.

I watched with utmost curiosity as the old gent clambered over the rocks, baited with a hunk of fish, and, casting, lobbed this screwball thing out among the rocks. It slid down by its own weight, slipping among crevices. But because of its length and stiffness it went nowhere that it could not be pulled out. Suddenly there was a tug and the man set back hard on his stiff rod. The rockfish he had hooked tried, as I envisioned it, to run back into its hole. It was no go. The old codger reeled away and out came steel rod, fish, and all at the end of the line. I watched him work the device in kelp, too. It was a perfect solution to an insoluble problem. Occasionally he got broken off. He reached back then to his quiver, just as you or I would for another hook.

Since that time I have seen an adaptation of this idea that sprang from some other fertile brain. This is the way people fish for these same rock-loving species, using a long, stiff pole with no line and only a few inches of wire leader to which a baited hook is attached. They probe the pole itself down among the rocks. When a rockster bites, they have only to withdraw the pole.

The most gratifying aspect of "curiosa" fishing lore as a whole is that as all of us know the source never dries up. We continue endlessly to discover and contrive.

"I was lying under a tree by the river," a friend told me last summer, "with my head propped on my tackle box. I wanted to catch some bass and panfish but apparently they weren't feeding. Absently I watched a cow walking along munching grass, and behind her came a whole army of cowbirds, busily picking up the bugs she stirred from their hiding places. Instantly I had it."

What he had was an idea. He pulled on his waders and got into the stream. He tromped through every weed bed along the bank for some distance. Then he got out and walked the bank back to where his tackle lay. By now the place where he'd started the big stir-up had settled down. He eased in gently and began casting—and catching what he had come for.

In the same fashion mountain whitefish anglers in the West kick stones in the shallows above a pool to loosen nymphs. These float down and chum the lazing whitefish. Or, another angle on the same trick—an ancient one, actually, but one the present-day angler seldom knows about—is this. When trout or bass are lying inert on the bottom of a pool, on occasion stirring them up by hurling rocks among them will get results. They dart about and become active. Activity, once their initial fright has passed, causes the same reaction as exercise in a lethargic human: they suddenly feel an urge to eat.

The really astute angler can take a simple idea like this

chumming and activation business and make a production of it, using endless variations on the theme. One of the most comical, and effective, sequences of this sort I ever witnessed took place over a deep tidal pool off a mangrove island along the Gulf. I watched two anglers working together. Both wore Polaroid glasses. One stood methodically tossing out bait shrimp. The other was tensely ready with his rod. He was baited with shrimp.

I eased up and watched and it was plain that each time a shrimp was thrown out a number of small trout and reds rushed out of the dimness of deep water to fight over it. Then suddenly the fellow tossing shrimp said, "Now!" The other cast his bait. Instantly there was a rousing strike, right at the surface. He was into a tremendous specimen. Whether trout or red I could not tell.

Unfortunately the big brute was lost. But they explained to me something I already knew, having tried a similar trick on other species at times. "The small ones come barreling out to grab a bait," one said, "and the big boy we'd seen down there gets mad over it. We didn't want to ruin things by letting any little ones get hooked. So we baited them until Mr. Big came tearing in to shoulder the others aside. A cast right then will almost always get him!"

There's really no way to end a discussion of this kind. The material itself is endless. Remember how many times you have read or heard that a fish eye makes a good bait? It has been used effectively for many years. The famed Optic flies of some years ago followed this general idea. Later a research organization came up with results of a study project tending to prove that predator fish target in on the eye of their forage. A lure manufacturer began making a lure that was practically all eye.

In another area of research anglers I know are probing the mysteries of color from fresh angles—the spectrum as related to water depth and clarity. I remember once explaining to someone that marine fish of deep water are often bright red, and that ichthyologists suspect this is because blending of red with existing deepwater greens makes these species appear gray, thus less visible to predator species. By the same token, colored lures change color or disappear the deeper they go, depending upon what light rays, long or short, penetrate to them.

Does a red lure disappear entirely as it sinks, and if so at what depth in water of a given clarity? Does green show up best at far depths, with orange and yellow going the way of red on the way down? Do the blues, indigos, violets last longest? Is visibility alone, because of color, a solid factor in why fish at varying depths do or do not strike lures? Notes of mine show that fishermen friends — not scientists, just average anglers — were pondering and experimenting this way twenty years ago. Today several gadgets are marketed that let a sensing probe down to any given depth up to 100 feet or more, and show on a dial what the light measures there. They also tell which lure color should be used at the selected depth, for best visibility.

Such are the endless obscure paths of knowledge, deep and shallow, that we fishermen endlessly explore. None of us will ever be able to gather all the scattered knowledge. But we can each keep learning, gathering, passing along. Indeed, learning the wondrous ways of fishermen is in itself half the fun of fishing.

2
Never Catch a Muskie!

Tom Hennessey and I were sitting on the porch of his cabin on the hillside above his backwoods Wisconsin lake. We could look down the short slope to the water. Here a white birch leaned, reflecting, and a crisscross of submerged logs lay in the tamarack-stained water among lily pads in the shade of the slanted tree. To the left Tom's small dock jutted.

A family of six black ducks, mother and partly grown young, came gliding along, disappeared under the dock, reappeared on the other side near the submerged logs. Tom groaned.

"They never learn," he said. "Originally there were ten."

One youngster dawdled behind. There was a wild roil of water. The others squawked and skittered away. Where the laggard had been there were only expanding rings from the sudden surface disturbance.

"The dirty damn brute!"

"Lord, man," I blurted, "that's a *monster* muskie! Let's try him!"

I was already up, grubbing for tackle. But Hennessey said, "I don't *want* to catch the cussed fish. Eight years I've owned this. Bet I've made fifty thousand casts. Never caught one yet. I've seen guys go through this muskie thing and finally catch one. You think it's bad beforehand? Ha! I've quit!"

I went down to the dock, began casting a jointed plug. Funny. I knew exactly what Hennessey meant. It had happened to me. I'd caught a number of muskies. The years, the anguish it had taken! I made a dozen casts. Nothing.

"The big devil just ate a duck," I told myself, making the usual excuses. "That's why he won't hit."

I was remembering an old guide I'd often fished with. "How do you catch a muskie?" exasperated anglers would ask him. "Cast ten thousand times," he'd say.

"Maybe," I thought, "he spit out the duck." I started casting again, counting.

At one hundred sixteen I saw movement. It was the muskie. BIG! Lazing along behind my lure, following. They never hit when they do this, just never. But—maybe *this* time it would be different. I cast sixty-six more times. My arm ached. I despised the fish.

Hennessey shouted, "I got the booze out and ice ready. Come have a juice. You'll crack up."

I cranked in, walked up, sat with Tom, sipping. He was right. I wished I'd never caught that first one. It's the worst thing that can happen to a man.

Indeed, thousands of anglers have told themselves that. They've spent hundreds of thousands of dollars catching no muskies, a hundred times that catching a few. This fish is the one authentic freshwater enigma. The only man I ever knew who really had the whammy on 'em brought in record after record. It turned out he had never caught a single muskellunge. He was getting them from an old Indian who illegally netted them. All his friends reviled him. Frankly, I thought he had a great idea. It worked!

The truth is, you see, nobody knows how to catch muskellunge. If a guide tells you he does, don't book him. Many persons think they know how—for a day or two at a time. In fact, the whole intriguing quality of muskie fishing is the romance, the lovely torture, the mesmerism of not knowing.

"It hurts awful," a wildly frustrated friend once told me, "but it hurts awful good—ain't that hell?"

Once during ten days I fished with four crack guides. Each told me precisely what to do, and guaranteed success. Each fished with me, too. We caught nothing. Each explained why—too cold, too hot, too early, too late, too dark, too light. Disgusted, I went to a small lake where no muskies were known, tried to relax by fishing for walleyes with a bobber and some two-inch minnows. Muskies never fool with such puny forage. Bait's gotta be big. Guides, and the books, all say so. I say so, too. But the first fish I hung was a muskellunge that jumped and looked like 30 pounds, and tore me up before I could get my jaw flapped shut. The moral is, don't think you know, because not even the muskie knows what it will do. And, as most muskie guides will agree, muskies are exceedingly individual fish. You'll catch the second one doing everything you learned not to do catching the first one!

Of course, years of muskie fishing have produced a few basic techniques that apparently come closer than others to assurance of success, and these are the methods I intend to

17

comment on. None is remotely infallible. None works until the muskie is ready. All writing about muskellunge speaks of them as "moody" fish. Translated, this means the writer doesn't know when the muskie will be ready. It may be tomorrow, or next year. The muskie doesn't know, either. Start with this knowledge and you are already ahead, armed with patience, resignation, fatalism. But meanwhile you may as well try to learn *something*.

First you must understand what sort of fish this is. It is unfortunate that pike and muskies look rather similar, and are in the same family. Pike fishermen get thinking the two are alike. They're not. Pike are fun, but stupid. Muskies are either more intelligent, or more stupid. Nobody knows which. Pike will gang up in a good spot. Muskies are almost invariably solitary when grown. Pike may be scattered over a large expanse of water. Muskellunge, with few exceptions, lie one at a time and fairly widely spaced along a lake or stream border, in very specific spots. Again with few exceptions, during fishing season they will be in shallow water — 4 to 15 feet — near shore, always in or near cover.

This cover may be weeds, but in general such weeds will be surface cover to give at least dappled shade, and below surface not especially dense. This is a big creature. It needs maneuvering room. A small underwater "hill" out in a lake, offering a hundred or so square yards of weed canopy very shallow in center and perhaps 4 feet deep at edge of the weeds, then dropping quickly to deep water on all sides, hopefully with a few rocks and a soft bottom, is perfect. So are small coves of larger bays, protected, calm, with shade from shore and with submerged down timber. If it is jack-strawed just below surface, more open beneath, it is excellent. In a few specialized muskie habitat situations, rocky bars in medium-deep water may be hangouts, or rocky

Muskellunge top, pike center, hybrid bottom. Muskies and pike may look a lot alike, but their behavior is quite different, and muskies are much harder to catch.

stream pools. These might be examples in the Great Lakes, and in Tennessee streams.

There are many other varieties of muskie hangouts, but this gives a general picture. Think of the mature muskie as having a lair. It lives for long periods — a whole season, maybe season after season — in this precise spot. Surrounding the specific lair it has a domain. It is not basically a cruiser, a

19

roamer. The domain is limited, its base the lair, its borders somehow understood by the fish itself and seldom overlapping the bailiwick of another muskie of comparable size, although it may usurp rights of smaller fish. It may even gobble them up. Fishermen have rather commonly found floundering muskellunge, one attempting to swallow another more than half as large as itself.

Because a muskellunge is big, it "eats big." This is the rule. You can't make positive statements about muskellunge, but you can be sure it will usually want a large bait or lure. When it swallows a large fish the period required for digestion and assimilation is quite long. Thus feeding periods when muskies are really ready may be widely spaced and not readily predictable. Pike, for example, more commonly take several smaller fishes rather than one large one. The muskie is a lurker, but small stuff usually does not interest it. If your lure or bait happens to appear at the proper moment, whammo. If the muskie swallowed a one-pound fish just an hour, or five minutes, previously, probably you'll be ignored. Maybe until tomorrow. This is why constant, long-term, stubborn casting eventually pays off.

Muskellunge seem to have preferences in forage fish, but these may be only because of availability. Suckers are standard because suckers are resident in scores of muskie waters and thus a readily available source of food. Walleyes, also in many muskie waters, are much relished, and where it is legal to use them they are excellent bait. I know of two cases where muskies grabbed walleyes fishermen were bringing in, and in each case the muskie, allowed to swallow the walleye, was also landed. This is because the muskie swallows its forage fish headfirst. A walleye goes down easily, but, protesting, raises its spiny fins and cannot be disgorged. Muskies eat many other varieties. I know one lake where they are commonly found with big bluegills in

Casting a dead, trussed sucker for muskies. Suckers are part of the muskie's usual diet.

their gullets. The lake has many of these. I once helped cut open a muskellunge in Michigan and we took from its stomach a 17-inch rainbow trout.

So, this is the kind of fish a muskellunge is. It eats other things, too, such as ducks. In Wisconsin and elsewhere, ducks even to maturity are sometimes decimated by muskellunge. At Tom Hennessey's place, before I left, I photographed the last two of that flock of nine immature blacks plus the mother. Tom wrote me later that the muskie got the final pair in my picture.

Spring and fall are the most active times for the muskellunge. You should go at those times if you can. If not, certainly you should not write off other times, because unpredictability is the muskie's middle name. As an example, I have long seethed over an experience in Wisconsin a few years ago. In late July I fished a small lake for a week without a strike. It was known to contain a large muskie population. I fished hard. I raised not a single fish. The next week I rowed a friend who had never fished for muskellunge.

It was a bad time of year. I kept saying that, probably to excuse my lack of success. We fished the first day without success. The second day we started about noon—a bad time of day to try for muskies, everyone always says, including me. In two hours the totally inexperienced gent hooked, jumped, and lost six good fish! I have no explanation. Certain lakes—it happened on a Minnesota lake one summer a few years ago—suddenly have a veritable explosion of muskie activity in midsummer, while lakes all around them are dead. Many explanations are offered. Actually, nobody knows why.

Most muskie fishermen use big plugs, or large bucktails with spinners. This is not the most reliable method for taking muskellunge, as we'll see, but it is intriguing, and sporty. *Where* you cast is probably more important than other considerations. Most fishermen do too much casting where no fish lies. Knowing a small lake in detail, pinpointing known muskie lairs, is far better than indiscriminately casting. The lure must come close to the fish, because the fish is not going to chase after it from a long distance. Don't confuse this with a "follow." Muskies follow a lure so often you'll want to break your damn rod. But they follow a lure that has landed or passed close to their lair. Pinpoint casting to the most likely spot in a cove, and with great accuracy, is important. So is repetition. I once made over fifty casts into a small area that looked good, because I had seen a swirl behind the lure on the first cast. I finally got the strike. I also lost the fish.

How you handle the lure may be more important than the lure itself. Here again, please, no infallibles. But by and large a muskellunge, unless it strikes immediately upon the appearance of the lure, is slow to make up its mind, or to decide. A swiftly retrieved lure discourages it. Remember, muskellunge are extremely efficient killers. They may be hungry but they are seldom desperate. They can wait for the easy kills. Coax, tease, make the lure wiggle, let it bob to the surface—a diving plug is best because of this—start it, stop it, race it briefly. Short jerks and wiggles of a jointed plug are an excellent technique.

In fact, the jointed plug, one of the most successful of muskie artificials, is probably the best idea of its kind ever concocted. Not just for appealing action. For every ten muskies that strike artificials of all kinds, it's doubtful if more than three are hooked. Of those, hardly one in ten is landed. They're hard-mouthed. It's difficult to get the hooks hung solidly enough in such a powerful brute. But the record on jointed plugs and bucktail-spinner combos is better than average. That's why these are considered top lures. Actually, the reason they land more fish is that they hook them better. A bucktail seized by a muskie is almost certain to stick. A jointed plug flops and bends and grabs. Plugs with hooks hung out at the sides on steel wire do likewise.

Nobody has ever asked me, but I will volunteer the information here to all lure makers—and sue the first one who steals the idea!—that plug makers have been wrong for years in their conception of muskie lures. For example, there have been several plugs a foot or more long made locally here and there in muskie country that have caught a lot of muskies—and lost one heck of a lot more. The ones I've seen and used have had wonderful action that intrigued muskellunge. But a long, stiff, heavy wooden plug doesn't get its hooks home easily, is easily ripped out and thrown. Furthermore, a striking muskie knows darned well the moment it clamps down that this is no fish. It tries instantly to let go.

In addition, muskies are known and have actually been seen to smash and rake a forage fish, sending a shower of blood and scales roiling into the water but dropping the mortally hurt victim immediately. Then the muskie will sidle up, seize it again, swim lazily away to its lair and swallow it. So

23

someday somebody will make a great big soft mushy diving-type plug, maybe of closed-cell plastic or rubber. The muskie will smash it, will like the feel and be fooled momentarily by it, and meanwhile the hooks, as the fish mashes down to immobilize its kill, will flip around and clamp into it from two or three angles and I'll be darned if he'll go free!

There's another "when" to muskie fishing besides the stated best-chance periods of spring and fall. Early morning and late afternoon are generally conceded to be the quality periods of any twenty-four hours. They are productive, but I would argue whether they are necessarily best. Fishermen have been saying they are so long they believe it. They get tired by breakfast time and quit. They start out late in the p.m. again. So, that's when they get action. A guy with guts enough to stay with it all day will catch his muskie just as I've said, when the *muskie* is ready, and it may be ready at any minute of any hour. I mean, *any* hour. That gets us to something unique.

Two muskie fishermen with whom I've been acquainted over the years have been convinced that it is not true, as most books and guides say, that muskies feed only by day.

"Guides say it," one of these men told me, "because they're too lazy to work at night. Scientists say it because they work days and write nights."

I fished with both of the gentlemen in question, and both proved several times that muskies can be taken in pitch dark. Both of them used plugs, because they had to fish by feel and obviously could feel the strike.

One of them used a black plug. He has caught a lot of muskies on it when darkness was so complete he couldn't have found his face with both hands. I've personally always thought the black-plug business was mumbo-jumbo, conversation malarkey, because the guy also guided some and it sounded to clients like real expert stuff. Nonetheless, success is hard to defy. So, after-dark plugging is definitely worth a try.

Now to the next method. Although it's not very sporty, there's no doubt trolling is the closest to a sure way to catch

A big one, hooked at night on a jet-black lure. The billy club lying on the seat was used before handling the fish like this; a muskie is quite an adversary in a boat.

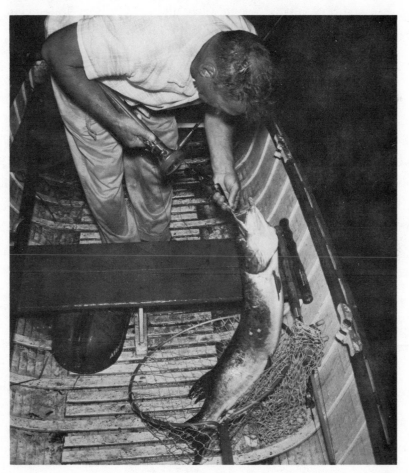

a muskellunge. A good indication is that it's not legal on all muskie waters. Trolling covers much water and also presents a lure much of the time in the best manner, if properly accomplished, and with the least physical effort. The troller circles around and around, close to shore, passing the lure near every watching fish in the lake, time after time. Furthermore, a muskie that follows a lure isn't spooked by coming to line's end and seeing a fisherman.

In fact, it is very possible that a muskie follows a cast lure and turns away not only because it sees boat and angler but because it sees them before the lure has left the limits of its domain. The sight of the angler simply inhibits decision. A trolled lure, followed, starts to leave the vicinity and the fish makes the decision to belt it before it crosses the outer borders of its bailiwick. Many expert muskie men are convinced this is what happens.

Many also believe trolling artificials is better than trolling bait. As a rule, bait requires giving instant slack at the strike, then letting the fish have time to start swallowing the prey. With artificials, a fish is either hooked or missed right then. However, successful or not, trolling in my estimation is dull, impersonal, and requires little wit or ingenuity. The muskellunge deserves something better.

Paradoxically, the least sporting method of catching a muskie is the one most fraught with anticipation, tension, and excitement, and is, next to trolling, probably the most successful. This is still-fishing, drifting, or paddling very slowly using a rig consisting of a big cork several feet below which a foot-long live sucker (or other baitfish) is rigged with a hook. Oddly, modern anglers too often consider bait-and-bobber an inane endeavor, a corny button-shoe pursuit. Truth is, for sustained pure drama nothing else in angling remotely compares.

For instance, there was this June day on tiny Tamarack

Lake back in the north-Minnesota brush. On that morning my guide, Larry Pinchot, had shown up with an evil grin and four suckers in a live-box.

"Today," he'd said, "we'll hang one big son!"

Now, jacketed against the crispness of spring air, we drifted through a channel between shore and a small island, a perfect place for a muskie to reside. Thirty yards behind us an unpainted cork big as an orange slithered from side to side, darted under, bobbed up as the lively tethered sucker sashayed. Were we lazing and lolling? Ho! We were hawk-eyeing that cork, jumping as if jabbed by a cattle prod every time it went under. This is the great excitement of cork fishing, especially for big fish. You never know what's going on down there. Suspense simply crackles.

Presently we were out of the channel, curving along over deeper water near shore. Larry said, "Guess he wasn't there."

The cork bobbled and started toward us, speeded up, stopped, jiggled, went down, stayed too long, then popped up. "Cripes," Larry said. "Do you suppose. . . ."

I did. For now the cork went under and moved off. Tensely Larry payed out line. The cork did not reappear. Line kept moving. A muskie had seized our sucker.

We were trembling. Yet excitement was only beginning. The reason was that with many fish at this juncture the hook might have been rammed home. But muskies are crazy critters. Sometimes they glom the bait. More often they hold it crosswise in their big nail-studded yap. When to set? Nobody ever knows. Strike too soon and you take it away. Maybe the fish will grab again. Usually it won't. Wait too long and the muskie will decide to spit it out rather than swallow it.

The cork came up, way out. Then it went down again and started taking line. Larry handed me the rod. He paddled quietly, hurrying to keep up. We didn't want a long line out for the strike. The fish went clear around the island at a steady pace. In the channel it reversed and went back the other way, then headed into the lake. Ten minutes had passed.

"I can't stand much more," I murmured. I was shaking.

Larry grinned. "I've followed the cussed things half an hour—then had 'em drop it!"

Suddenly motion stopped. The cork stayed down. Nervously Larry whispered, "He's on a bar out there. Get ready. He's swallowing it."

"You sure?" I whispered.

Larry exploded. "Hell no, I ain't sure! Mebbe he ain't swallowing it. I'm only a guide." Then he laughed. "Cripes, get it over. Okay? Ram him. Better or worse."

I snugged up, raised my backside off the seat, reached the rod forward, then came back and really rammed him. WOW! He had it. Line was torn from the reel, the fish shot up and along the surface, throwing water, then took to the air. After that things were blurry, trying to keep him out of snags, hold him, get line around the boat as he raced. He was no monster but he was a wild one. At last we boated him. He weighed 22½ pounds.

While live-bait fishing for muskellunge is awesomely dramatic, the method most ingenious of all is casting a dead sucker or other similar bait. It requires tremendous craft and adeptness and judgment. I think often nowadays that we lose perspective in our modern world as to what are the true *skills* in outdoor sports. The wealthy gentleman who fishes off Peru for a world-record billfish is lauded as a great fisherman. He may be a top-shape athlete but he doesn't even need to be, and usually isn't even remotely, a fisherman. Anybody who can afford it can match him. The big billfish is naive and unafraid, and besides that the guide goes through

28

all the necessary motions, including cashing the check. The country kid, wise with observations drawn from experience in his small domain, who crawls on his belly to the edge of a brook and by sheer craft removes a wary old speckled trout from beneath a cutbank is the real fisherman! The differences between the muskie troller and the one who trusses and casts a dead bait are similar.

The bait used is generally a fish of about a pound. With stout cord it is tied behind the gills and around the snout — this is one reason suckers are recommended, because the snout has a tough ring at its end — so that scores of casts may be made with a single bait without tearing it free. Ahead of the snout the big hook is rigged, much the same as with a live sucker. The method makes a stiff rod mandatory. The work is tiring, because heaving a one-pound sucker hour after hour is simply hard physical labor. Such a bait is difficult to cast at a low angle. Besides, it is intended to land with a loud *splatt,* to attract attention of a muskellunge. Thus, it is cast in an extremely high arc as a rule. Obviously, this makes accuracy possible only with much practice and expertness.

The best way to learn how to truss and cast a dead bait is to go a couple of times with a guide who is good at it and be taught first-hand. If you happen to catch a fish, or see one caught during this period, I can promise you, you will be an addict. The method is very active, and very exciting. Casting should be pinpoint. The theory is that a hungry muskie will see or hear the splash and think a baitfish has rolled or else been slashed at by some other marauder trespassing on its domain. It rushes in and seizes the bait.

Sometimes the strike swiftly follows the splash. If there is no strike then, the bait is reeled in, with short jerks and varied maneuverings, to give it the realistic action of a crippled sucker. For it to ride properly — that is, on an upright keel – it must be trussed exactly right. Skill again. Regardless of when the strike comes, the muskie presumably assumes that it has immobilized the bait. The fisherman must instantly give slack. Now the same process starts as when a live sucker is used. The muskie carries its "kill" off and eventually either swallows it, or drops it – and you guess which, and also when you should send the hook home!

A most amazing scene to witness is a big muskellunge coming to meet the flying sucker. Oh yes, it occurs. Old hands will tell you. You won't believe it until you see it. I have seen it.

There was this big birch log, submerged a few feet, on the shore of a lake not far from the Wisconsin-Michigan border. My guide was spelling me. I am no great shakes at dead-bait casting but I try. And I was weary. Not a strike all day. He urged me to take the rod again to make the cast to this log.

"There's been a big one here all season," he said. "He lies somewhere below that log. I've had him swirl at lures three times, but have never jabbed him."

I shook my head. I was discouraged and so beat I just didn't care – or so I thought that second. He heaved the sucker. It went high in the air, moved in a long, wide arc, and fell precisely where he had planned, which seemed impossible, right beside the log. That is, it was aimed and falling exactly there. I was watching the bait and as it started down I was conscious of a tremendous swirl far inshore toward the base of the log. A great fish shot along the surface, creasing water so that its back showed, and so swiftly it seemed to be a dozen feet long.

As the sucker struck the water the fish blotted out the space in a vicious, breath-catching lunge that threw spray several feet high. There was no question whatever that the muskie had seen the bait coming down from above, had shot forth to pinpoint the exact spot where it would land. The brute had the bait almost before it was wet. Some may choose to disbelieve this tale. No matter. I have witnessed the phenomenon three different times. You can find numerous guides who have seen the same thing happen.

On this occasion the guide was so startled he muffed it. Muskies shake up the best of them. Impulsively he struck. He hooked the muskie, too. Apparently it had struck so hard it got hook and all into its maw. It shot out of the water in a near-frightening display of power and wildness. On the second jump it went free. I did not feel badly at having missed the chance. I'm sure I, too, would have been too shaken to have given slack instantly.

These, then, are the fundamentals of muskie fishing lore. Other fishermen may have variations. These are the basics that seem most successful. But don't get the idea I am recommending muskie fishing. Having set these down, I think again of sitting on Tom Hennessey's summer-cottage porch, sipping my drink and wishing I had never caught that first one. However, as you read this, there's a good possibility that, like a fool, I will be fishing somewhere for a muskellunge. Thus it seems a little ridiculous, what I am going to say. For your own good, I think you should lay off it. Go be an alcoholic or something. It's far less frustrating. You can *always* come by a case of booze!

3
Blue Runners:
Dynamite on Light Tackle

It was midafternoon when we saw the birds, a skyful of them — gulls, pelicans, terns, all calling, wheeling, diving in a frenzy of excited feeding. Granger swung the boat around and headed straight for them, giving the motor all she'd take. It was a race, let me tell you. Cruisers were streaming toward us from every direction. Within fifteen minutes there were a dozen cutting circles around us, courses crossing and recrossing.

Small baitfish, driven to the surface, chopped to pieces by hordes of finned predators from below, came popping out by thousands. They skittered in sheets, throwing countless raindrops of spray behind them, along the tops of the swells.

The birds scooped them up from above. Lines, lures, boats slashed through them in the center.

At the rail where I stood, almost within arm's length I saw a thrilling picture. Blobs of silvery blue slashed by so fast the eye actually could not identify them. The speed of many an ocean predator is awesome to contemplate. Some of these I knew were mackerel. But many more I was positive were not. The fish were everywhere, sizzling along through the swells, leaving the water in twos, threes, dozens, like stabs of bright light swift as a camera shutter, a blizzard of feeding fish.

I was so interested watching that I missed one strike, and then another. Granger and Ferguson each had fish on, had them flopping over the side and into the fish tub.

"Big mackerel on!" one of them shouted again.

"I've got one, too!"

"Me, too!" I yelled.

Rods were flailing, bending — but no, when the streaking quicksilver fighters came aboard, they weren't mackerel but blue runners. The tub was filling fast now. We picked up a small mackerel here and there, about fifteen all told, not much for size. I had just started wondering what we were going to do with all those fish when the school sounded. The action ended as abruptly as it began.

Back at our dock, we sent out the call for anyone who wanted fish for dinner. We shared our mackerel. But there remained the blue runners I'd been worrying about, stacked high, with no takers.

Now the blue runner, for those who may not know about it, is a fish belonging to the family of saltwater jacks. Its average size is from 1 to 2 pounds, with an occasional fish up to 6 pounds of fighting dynamite. Though a bit more streamlined than the blocky jack crevalle, it has the same powerful forked tail. The bony shields running down the rear portion of its lateral line, near the tail (common in all of the jack family), run much farther forward than in the common jack. The blue runner's fin arrangement is similar to that of the jack crevalle, but the pectorals and ventrals are dull, near colorless, not yellow as in the crevalle. Unquestionably hundreds of thousands of blue runners have been caught without much comment by saltwater fishermen, all the way from Cape Cod south. Around the Florida Peninsula the runners are one of the most common of fishes. I'll peg them right now as one of the most fantastic fighters going. But by and large, it is one of those species which has had little close attention paid to it. It is just a fish you happen to catch when fishing for something else. And of course, with a great variety of larger game fish abounding in the same waters, it is difficult for the blue runner to get a serious hearing.

In addition, the blue runner has the jack crevalle to thank—or hold a grudge against!—for its poor reputation as an eating fish. The jack crevalle is edible, but strong and bloody. Very few people eat it. Still fewer can honestly say they like it. And it is rather generally taken for granted, even by natives who should know better, that the blue runner is as poor eating as the jack. It looks like a jack—it *is* a jack, actually—so why bother with it?

I admit I was taken in too. In all my winters around Southern salt waters, I had never yet heard a word about the blue runner as a table fish. But when I saw the noses turned up at them on the dock, I couldn't live with my conscience. I can never feel it's right and proper to kill anything you do not intend to use. I picked up a few of the solid little gamesters, cut off head and tail, cleaned the body cavity. Leaving the leathery skin on, I toted them back to the trailer.

Ravenous, I sat down to a dinner of broiled Spanish mackerel and trimmings, fairly drooling. We waded through

The blue runner is a relative of the jack crevalle, but is more streamlined.

the mackerel in a hurry. Gosh, they were small. Meanwhile, in the broiler, the little blue runners sizzled away. My wife, Ellen, had not split them. They were pretty small for that. She simply broiled them in their hides, turning them over occasionally.

She brought the blue runners to the table and carried away the bones of the mackerel. We looked at each other, both of us still hungry.

"Well," she said, "have you lost your nerve? You brought them home, you know."

"All right," I said, "I'll try one if you will."

Almost timidly, since neither of us cares for really strong fish, we each slipped a crisp-jacketed blue runner onto a plate. I started to slide a knife under the skin, and found to my amusement that the skin was already loose. "Like baked potatoes," I said. "You just peel 'em. Slips right off."

Amusement changed to amazement when we stared at the meat as the shuck of leathery skin slid away. It was not dark and bloody, with a fishy stench, like the jack crevalle. Rather it was light, and tempting in smell. We each took tentative bites, then looked at each other with pleasantly shocked surprise.

"Well I'll be danged!" I said. "It's absolutely delicious." To this day I'll gladly trade six Spanish mackerel, and throw in a pompano to boot, for a healthy serving of blue runners.

At another spot on the coast, we decided to hole up and really have at 'em. Equipped with a freshwater trout rod and an ample single-action reel with some backing on, just in case, I slipped a little auto-top boat into the water of a quiet bay and went hunting. I had very successfully used a red-and-yellow streamer with a silver-tinsel body on jacks, during another winter. That, I reasoned, should do the trick, if I could locate the fish.

I cruised the secluded bay freckled with mangrove islands, looking for birds. Finding a group of feeding pelicans, I drifted down into them, and shot the streamer out on a long cast. The difficulty with this kind of fishing is the speed with which one must retrieve. Most of the open-water fish in salt water disdain a lure that moves too slowly. A spinning outfit is perfect—but I like to fly-fish. I began stripping line in long, swift pulls, letting it fall into the bottom of the boat. There was an instant, furious hit that kinked the rod into a half-circle and made me wince at the strain. The line on the boat bottom sizzled out, caught on something, and that was all. My streamer was gone.

I didn't even know what I had hung. For half an hour, I kept trying without luck. Then I cranked up and started hunting again. By now the tide was running, going out of the bay. Things should be hot—if I could find the place. Between two tiny islands of mangrove I saw half a dozen pelicans hesitate, then wheel and come plummeting. I shot the boat ahead toward the spot.

What a natural! Here a narrow, shallow bar strung between the two islands. Tidewater was pouring over the bar like a swift river. Just off the bar, hemmed in by the islands, was a deep blue hole, churning with the run of the tide. And on its surface sparkled a blaze of shimmering silver, lit by the bright sun glinting off thousands of baitfish harassed violently from below.

I was out of the boat, tossing my anchor, and wading into position on the bar before the little craft had come to a full stop. Peeling line, I shot a new streamer on a tough leader straight out into the deep-blue swirl before me. I gave the line one strip — and had it literally ripped from my left hand. Grabbing frantically, I managed a new hold. I hardly dared try to stop the run. Line raced across my fingers. The rod was down in a fine, snug bend, tip vibrating wildly, and far out there over the blue water in the churning wake of the fish tiny bait species skittered across the singing line. About then a miniature ax blade of glinting silver and blue went slapping across the surface.

My first fly-rod blue runner was on, and fighting beautifully!

It is always amazing how strong saltwater fish are, and doubly so when you hook up to one of the members of the jack or mackerel clan. I was sure the blue runner would weigh no more than 2 pounds, if that, yet on my light tackle it was giving an astonishing performance.

Some years after that first fly-rod encounter, I just digress to say, I got into an enormous school at the end of the ship channel at Port Aransas, Texas. This time I was in a boat, and using standard freshwater spinning tackle. The rip at the end of the jetty, where the channel meets the Gulf, was churning in a blow. The Gulf was too rough to get out far into. Terns swept incessantly over the rip, and small bait-fish were popping out everywhere, indicating predators down below.

We trolled, crisscrossing the rip, using an odd lure born in Port Aransas years back and called the Hootie. It is nothing but a hook on a wire leader, clothed in a scanty mop of thin net string. No weight is used. The Hootie simply

These fish, all about 2 pounds, were caught on the Texas coast with a bait-casting lure called the Hootie.

skitters along the surface or barely beneath. I was rigged with two of them. We soon discovered that the predator fish were blue runners, and all of about 2 pounds each. That's big! When one whacked the Hootie it was just all I could do to handle it on the freshwater-bass-weight spinning tackle. And when on three occasions I got a two-runner hookup they'd take line so fast we had to back the boat down on them to crank up. They literally ruined the freshwater reel I was using in about half an hour.

Blue runners do not leap. And I discovered when first fly-fishing for them—and later while using the near-weightless Hootie—that the stubborn little devils, with no lure or lead weight to hold them down, fought much more at the surface than they did when caught by usual trolling methods. They'd go careering along throwing spray, or heel over time after time atop a swell.

The fly rod, of course, was the most fun, and that first session a great thrill. With no boat speed to hinder them, no broomstick rod to inhibit them, they were terrors to handle. I braced my feet on that first one, took a high grip, so that the rod butt would rest against my wrist and help relieve the strain. But my hand and arm were trembling and I had to change hands with the rod before the racing, everywhere-at-once fish was even half subdued.

At last I had him in. Netless, I reached down and seized him. It has been a long time since I've felt so proud of a fish. I chuckled at my own pride in this catch—why, the blighter was way under 2 pounds! Mentally, I went over all the species I had ever caught on a fly rod. I am sure that, by weight, I have never hooked anything to compare with the speed, power and tenacity of the blue runner.

With a toss, I threw him into the boat. Then I shot the streamer out again. Stripping furiously, I had moved the lure little more than 10 feet when I was brought up with a jolt

Blue runners put up a good fight on light fly-fishing tackle. They strike streamers readily.

again. The strike of this fish is sensational. It is also tough on a light rod, especially when you are swiftly peeling in line. Without moving from my position on the bar, I caught a dozen. They had me about as worn out as I had any of them.

There was only one handicap that I could see, and it was a pleasant one. It took so long to lick each fish that with such tackle a fellow could never fill any tub while a heavy feeding period lasted! The baitfish subsided into the deep water, the bar began to show as the tide ran down. I knew the action was over, but I made one more cast. The moment the streamer hit the surface, it was smacked. I saw the fish make his attack from at least a yard away. He shot through the surface water, throwing spray, moving so swiftly my eye could not follow, my reflexes could not reply. I had no time to strike. He chopped down on the streamer, turned, jerked the slack out—and cut me off clean.

It was my last streamer, the last blue runner for that winter. A short length of fine wire, I reflected, would proba- bly be a good idea between leader and fly. One thing I knew for sure, I was going to find out. I badly needed more dyna- mite like this!

40

4
How to Find
and Catch Trophy Bass

A friend who is a diligent and enthusiastic bass fisherman keeps a log on his catches. He kiddingly says that the 6-to-8-pounders showing here and there were some of the better culls caught while after the *real* trophies. The fact is, he has caught some authentic trophies, several of 9 and 10 pounds, one topping 13.

This man is what may be termed a "big-bass" fisherman. Skeptics like to believe he is lucky. Undoubtedly Lady Luck watches over him approvingly. But it is his carefully researched, modern scientific approach that makes him successful. He shuns small-bass situations, and proves repeatedly—just as many top tournament men do—that locating and taking trophy bass is chiefly a matter not of luck but of know-how.

The most interesting slant is that any bass addict can do quite well as a trophy taker. It is a matter of upping your odds by scrupulously adhering to certain rules. The *more* you fish, obviously the better your chances of scoring. *Where* you fish, geographically, will dictate what can be considered a true trophy.

Suppose, for example, that you live in Michigan and have little chance to travel outside your state. You can be properly proud of a largemouth of 7 or 8 pounds here, and you'll be really a bit lucky to land anything larger. If you can make periodic forays outside your home state, you can figure on adding 2 to 3 pounds for a top trophy taken in the mid-South, and 4 to 6 if you fish in the Deep South, Florida, or more recently, southern California, where Florida-strain bass are making waves.

To be sure, an 11-pound bass could turn up in the North, and a 14-pounder in Missouri. Odds, however, are against catching one. Reasons are that maximum size of bass depends—assuming the fish enjoy optimum living conditions—on two factors: length of annual growing season, and age. Few anglers realize that fish, unlike warm-blooded creatures, do not reach an adult growth and cease growing. Fish grow continuously until they die. Numerous influences, of course, dictate speed of growth. It is swifter up to and through the years of maturity and prime, slower thereafter. However, an unusually large bass is invariably a very old bass.

A bass that lives to be eight or nine years old is comparable to a man ten times that. Because fish are coldblooded, their metabolism slows as water temperature lowers. Growth of a Northern bass slows decidedly in fall, ceases altogether for some months in winter. In the mid-South the growing season is at least two or three months longer. In southern Florida it continues around the year. In fact, biologists find it impossible to age some Florida bass. Their scales show no growth rings because they grow continuously. Thus, assuming proper forage conditions, the size of an old (trophy) bass depends on latitude; the farther south, the larger. The few bass that prove exceptions to this rule are the ones that somehow happen to live well past the average life span. These are not common. Also, gentle climes give bass better odds of living to ripe old age than do severe Northern habitat conditions.

Whether you try for a trophy within your state, or branch out regionally or nationally, selecting the proper type of lake or lakes where you'll concentrate is of utmost importance. For example, I know a lake in northern Michigan considered one of the best bass lakes in the state. I personally have caught and released thirty or forty bass there in an afternoon. But I have never seen a bass over 3 or 4 pounds come out of that water. I know a dozen comparable lakes in Florida. They produce amazingly, but never fish of trophy size.

These lakes, and the hundreds like them, are invariably "bassy-looking." There are a lot of weed beds, lily-pad pockets, fringes of reeds. All are shallow lakes. Some Southern lakes that produce fantastic action have a maximum depth of no more than 15 feet. Scores of Northern lakes loaded with bass may go down in spots to no more than 20 or 25. Few trophy bass ever come from such waters. Probably 95 percent of all mounting-size bass, in any latitude, come from deep lakes, with depths of 50 to 75 feet or more.

For example, lakes such as Eufaula in Oklahoma, its namesake in Alabama, Table Rock in Missouri, and Rayburn in Texas have given up astonishing numbers of trophies. It's not difficult to find depths of 100 feet or more in any of these lakes. Not that you'll catch your big ones at 100 feet. But

This small Florida lake did not look very "bassy." Cover was sparse and it was deep. But it contained real trophy bass.

Deep, clear, rocky lakes—this is Table Rock in Missouri—are often better than weedy ones.

A candidate for the wall—a full 12 pounds of largemouth. It was caught by design, not luck.

Underwater photo of bass caught on deep-running lure.

numerous statistical records show that the big ones mostly come from large, deep lakes, scads of smaller fish from shallow lakes.

When scouting for deep lakes, don't search necessarily for weedy ones that look like what you imagine a hot bass lake should. Excessively fertile habitats usually teem with varied fish and aquatic life. The "busy" habitat is inclined to high production, but few spectacular specimens. The trophy-bass lake is usually one of only modest fertility and clear, deep water. There may be fewer fish, and their growth rate may even be a bit slower than in the extremely fertile lake. However, it is a well-authenticated rule of nature that life expectancy in such environments is longer than in teeming habitats. There's a fair chance that a high percentage of the bass will live to reach old age.

I recall a Southern lake I fished not long ago. It is one of the least bassy-looking lakes imaginable, at least compared to what average bass enthusiasts understand by that term. The shoreline has no submerged weed beds worth mention. There is a bit of drowned brush, a lot of maiden cane thrusting from the water in shoreline patches. The water is clear and deep, the bottom slants steeply down from the cane areas. Water temperature on a year-round basis is a few degrees lower than in other lakes of the area. But this one is a superb big-bass lake. It never produces a lot of fish. I doubt it carries a heavy population. But when you do hang a bass, you are almost certain to have a good one.

An interesting aside concerns Florida's famous Lake Jackson. This is a big-bass lake. Studies on it tend to indicate, however, that survival of young bass is actually very low. Thus, young fish that do survive grow up in an uncrowded and not very competitive habitat, thereby attaining large size and good chances of longevity. Any comparable lake (where competing fish species are not out of balance) will invariably be a good lake for trophies.

The matter of species competition is important in lake selection. Compatible varieties such as crappies, bluegills or channel cats are seldom a problem in any sizable lake. But rough fish, from the gizzard shad of the South to various suckers, carp and buffaloes, commonly are. They swiftly usurp living room, destroy habitat, grow so fast small bass cannot take them. In the case of the shad, these seldom stay near shore even when small, and thus give young bass little chance to utilize them as forage. Any lake where rough fish are out of control is not worth wasting time on. For example, LBJ Lake in Texas was a few years ago an excellent big-bass lake. Finally an awesome imbalance of rough fish ruined it. When it was drawn down and a massive kill accomplished by biologists, the bass population was found to be almost nil.

46

In today's world of bass fishing one of the large impoundments is far and away the best choice for the average trophy hunter. To repeat, it should be clear, deep, and with no rough-fish problems. These large lakes invariably contain the most mature bass simply because of their size. If you know how to find them, your odds therefore are better than on smaller waters. There are certain rules for culling out impoundments not likely to give up trophies.

Brand-new impoundments won't do. The newly flooded, rich habitat will have hordes of small bass, few large ones. For an impoundment to "come of age"—reach peak bass production and maturity—requires four to seven years, depending upon latitude. Trophy hunting should begin about the fifth year. A lake just *past* its peak, beginning to taper off and stabilize as its bottom ages, may have the most real trophies. These are old bass from an early age class.

Years six, seven and eight may be best for this specialized fishing. Before or after, odds are higher. Occasionally an impoundment with all perfect attributes may produce bass of only modest size, even in the best years. If you hit one, move on. It's slated to be a dud.

The constant-level impoundment is the one to seek. Not all are. Those drawn down for irrigation or other purposes produce erratically. Drawdowns occurring at spawning time may destroy an entire age class of bass. A drawdown at any time disturbs and destroys food chains and the rich breeding ground of the shallows. They also force bass to move, then move again as water comes back. These unstable lakes turn out few trophies.

Knowing *where* a big bass is most likely to be in a lake sounds like the toughest part. Actually it's not that difficult. In any lake you can eliminate 75 percent or more of the entire expanse. The bottom over all of this will be virtually fishless. Some will be too deep, some devoid of cover. Some

47

will lack oxygen. Some will be mud, not favored by bass. The other 25 percent will be shoreline and all areas with cover—rocks, brush, trees, logs—down to about 45 feet. Of this, the trophy man can eliminate most shoreline. Certainly many fishermen operate here successfully, but seldom successfully for large bass, except along steep shoreline. You can eliminate areas where school bass hang out, too. This leaves no more than 10 to 15 percent of lake bottom to be searched.

It *is* the *bottom* you are interested in. Catching a mounting bass on top is rare, regardless of how enjoyable that type of fishing is. Bass are bottom fish most of the time. Old ones spend almost all their hours on bottom or near it. Most select layers 15 to 35 feet deep. These are often near a drop-off to much deeper water—along submerged rock ledges, the protected side of a point, along a submerged ridge or island, in a depression such as an old brushy creek bottom, on the outside of the curve of some bend.

Use of a depth sounder is very nearly mandatory. But don't be too eager when a group of bass is located. Occasionally fish even of 5 or 6 pounds gang up. The crotchety elders of 10 or 12 are almost always loners. When your sounder locates a bottom structure likely to hold bass, probe the roughest fringes meticulously. The old loner should be in a crevice, a cave, under a stump, in a submerged treetop or brush patch, hidden in a patch of weeds, or beneath a crisscross of logs. It has a lair. The spot will be difficult for the fisherman to get to. Make up your mind in hunting trophy largemouths to get hung often and lose plenty of lures.

Very seldom are these fish in the open. Seldom do they cruise extensively. The friend who keeps that log says he searches for bottom structures appealing to 5- and 6-pounders, then checks out fringe locations hard to get a lure into. He fishes pinpoint, right to the hiding places. Trolling is

48

worthless. If you fish straight down, jigging a spoon or plastic worm in short flutters on or near bottom, you have a better chance. An old, corpulent bass does not wish to chase far. He rushes out a few feet if necessary. But fish slowly. Give him time for decision. His habit is to ambush or waylay forage. Use full-sized or large lures. Tidbits are not for these fish.

Bass are often not every-day feeders. Large bass may go several days, then gorge. If you locate a spot that should hold a monster, try it a number of days before giving up. The lunker hunter must "think" like an old bass. To it, *comfort* is exceedingly important. This means, for one thing, staying within a narrow temperature range. Young bass commonly leave favorite temperature layers in eagerness to feed. Old bass do so less and less. Except in the North in the winter, where they have no choice, outside temperature spread will fall between 60 and 75 degrees. Within this range, look for big bass most often at depths where temperature is between 68 and 75.

It's interesting to note that recent feeding experiments indicate that bass grow most swiftly at temperatures 2 to 4 degrees *below* their maximum comfort range. Between 70 and 73 degrees any largemouth is at its best. But numerous mounting-size specimens come each season from waters that are, by standards there, rather cool, that is, just under 70 degrees. Further, it is the *winter* months throughout the South and mid-South that produce the greatest number of trophies. Few fishermen realize this. Conditions may not be as pleasant for the angler, but February and March are the prime months.

Depth and temperature are of course closely related. A water temperature gauge is as important as the depth finder. Devices to measure dissolved oxygen can also be helpful, although few fishermen are willing to go that far. However, basic knowledge of importance of oxygen rating (parts per million) in any given water is worthwhile. Plentiful oxygen equals supreme comfort and well-being for any bass, but especially for the large old gentleman bigmouth that dislikes moving much.

This is one reason why winter months in the South are best. The lower the temperature, up to a point, the more dissolved oxygen available. In the mid-60s, water supports several parts per million more than at summer highs up toward the 80s. In addition, oxygen content has great stability in winter, when plant photosynthesis is at low ebb and decomposition likewise. In that deep, cool, only mildly fertile lake perfect for growing trophies, oxygen content changes little. In the weedy, fertile lake, drastic ups and downs occur. In any lake containing green aquatic plants, large bass that are the most selective about comfort will be most active beginning in late afternoon. Oxygen content is highest then. This is especially true in quiet bays and arms where wind action is minimal. Dawn sees the least dissolved oxygen present, because photosynthesis has been dormant during the night. This is a time of many fish of modest size.

Light is also an important consideration. The eye of a bass cannot blink. Its muscles cannot react as efficiently as those of the human eye to diminished brightness. The older a bass, the less adaptable its eyes are and the more it shuns bright light. It clings more and more to dim recesses. This is one reason so many trophies come out of deep holes, and why large bass are often caught at full dusk or even at night.

Regardless of what time of day you fish, shun the light as the bass does. Fish always to the shady side of the hiding place, i.e. the bole of a large drowned tree. Fish the shady side of a point where rock ledges stair-step downward. If there's a shady area along a steep shoreline, and submerged cover below, select this spot in preference to the remaining expanse of sun-drenched shoreline.

These, then, are the basic rules for finding and catching bass worthy of the taxidermist. However, they won't suffice without proper tackle. A monster bass has a tough mug. Driving a hook home, especially in deep water, is difficult. It requires power, stiff rod, stout line. Also, once you have the fish hooked, you must attempt to haul it unceremoniously by brute force from its lair. It will balk. As soon as you get it clear, it will try mightily to go back. These bass do not jump much, nor rush immediately surfaceward as many youngsters do. They bore down and sulk.

Every year innumerable trophies are lost to whippy rods, spin reels with peashooter drags, and light lines. Use a quality casting reel with stout star drag. Use a rod of medium length, with sensitive but rugged tip. The stiff so-called worming rods are excellent. Use line of at least 20-pound test. Many trophy addicts go to 30-pound. When a bass takes, really rear back and sock it to him. Then don't slack off. As the hook sinks home, keep him coming.

"The chances of getting a mounting bass from lake bottom to your den wall," says the man who keeps the log on his big catches, "are directly proportional to the length of time between hooking a fish and getting it into the boat. The shorter the better. In this game, the sport is in finding the fish, not in playing it. The fisherman who really manhandles 'em is the one who gets to do the bragging."

5

Tennessee Tarpon:
The Skipjack Herring

Have you ever itched all winter to be off on a fishing trip, made the wish come true about April — and then found that when you reached your prize spot the highly touted game fish weren't hitting? Did you happen to make such a trip into the mid-South, maybe, after bass or walleyes, hitting it at a lousy time, but with your time limited? If it hasn't happened to you, it could, and probably will. So listen. . . .

Rod in hand, I was climbing down the rocks below Douglas Dam on the French Broad River when I noticed a fisherman who was tied into a good one. The swirling brown water shattered out in front of him, and a slash of silver hurtled upward with a wild, directionless lunge that sent it plunging end over end. The fish landed with a crack and shot

52

skyward once more, upside down, and its gills flared red. I hurried. The fish leaped again. Tumbled. Floundered. Bored down. Sent spray flying. It was a crazy, explosive species with which I was unfamiliar. It fought not with craft but with violent frenzy.

The fisherman held his bent rod hard, looked toward me and grinned. "I came to catch bait for big catfish," he said, nodding toward the 2-pound firecracker at the end of his line, "and it's so blamed much fun I can't quit."

"What is it?"

"Tarpon," he yelled. It did look and act like a miniature silver king. But this was fresh water, hundreds of miles inland. This was Tennessee. The man said, "Tennessee tarpon," and laughed. "Look at him jump! Hurry up! Get your lure in the water!"

Such was my introduction to an astonishingly game fish

Left: Close-up of the large-scaled, miniature-tarpon-like skipjack herring. Not really edible, it's a dynamic game fish. *Right:* This fish is the gizzard shad, a totally different species that should not be confused with the skipjack herring or golden or river shad, but sometimes is.

My very first skipjack herring puts up dramatic battle. An attribute of this unknown is its amazing staying powers and its agility on the hook. The close-up of one fish I caught shows well the similarity, in miniature, to the form of the tarpon.

which has somehow managed to live through several centuries of American sport fishing without enough publicity to let the average angler know it even exists. Yet it is found throughout much of the Mississippi Valley and along the Gulf Coast.

The fish I refer to is often called a skipjack. That's not a very good name, because at least a dozen different species of both salt and fresh water have picked up the same name, at least colloquially. But it's a name that has stuck. The official name given it by the American Fisheries Society is skipjack herring (*Alosa chrysochloris*). That's better, because it really is a herring. The term "skipjack" refers to the fact that the

Below: Douglas Dam on the French Broad River in Tennessee. The boats in the far background are after catfish, using golden shad for bait.

55

fish, an active type, often leaps and skips along the surface while feeding.

Other names one may hear are river herring, blue herring, and golden shad. The herrings and shads are of course all closely related. Most of the important species are of salt water, but among these are the well-known American or white shad and the hickory shad that are anadromous — that is, they make spawning runs up coastal freshwater rivers. The skipjack herring, or golden shad, is a whimsical sort that seems a bit uncertain where it should live. It is chiefly a species of large rivers of the mid-South, such as the Ohio and Tennessee and their numerous tributaries. But farther south it also lives along the Gulf in salt water and makes spawning runs up coastal rivers just like the other varieties.

Mixed in its schools almost anywhere may be other shads, such as the Ohio shad and the Alabama shad. However, technical identification won't be very important to the man who does the fishing. He'll be too busy!

Nonetheless, this slender, dynamic and streamlined fish should not be confused with the small, non-game gizzard shad that is so awesomely abundant in many Southern impoundments and large streams. The gizzard shad is a forage fish upon which bass and other game fish fatten. It is also a nuisance that too often becomes so abundant it crowds out the game varieties. Nor should you get your hopes up about making any delicious meals from a catch of skipjack herring. This rather handsome high-jumper with greenish, silver and golden hues can't be turned into gourmet dishes such as planked shad or shad roe, for which the American or white shad is so famous.

This 1-to-3-pound gentleman is about as edible as the tarpon it resembles in miniature. It is bony, oily and strong. The Tennessee tarpon, as some fly and spin fishermen around the TVA dams jokingly — and respectfully — call it, is indeed worthless as a food fish, and is used locally as bait, whole, for big blue cats. But it sure is a show-stopper of a game fish, given the opportunity.

I stood one day on some rocks in the middle of Tennessee's swift, ice-blue Clinch River, a few miles below Norris Dam. I was fly-fishing for white bass in the still, flat pool above and to the side of a small falls.

Water rolled in a round, surging crystal bulge over the lip of the falls, which dropped possibly 6 feet. Suddenly I was astonished to see a rise just above the lip of the cascade. Surely the foolish fish would be swept over the drop and smashed onto the rocks below. But a flashing streak of silver, too fast to follow well, shot back upstream.

I stopped fishing and watched. A big skipjack came speeding down, drawing a silver line through the blue water, headed toward the far corner of the little cataract. At the very last instant, with astonishing timing, it did a breathtakingly beautiful stunt. The long fish, with its immensely powerful forked tail, wheeled broadside and lanced across the rolling bulge of blue water. It was actually *over* the lip when it seized whatever small bit of food it had been chasing. Yet with a surge and a flick, it shot upward, knifing the falling water—upward and out of the danger zone, only to repeat the performance a few seconds later.

The skipjack herring eagerly seizes minnows, and it also takes some surface and aquatic insects. Watching the big one feeding at the lip of the falls, I got above it so that I could present a fly to it. I was using a medium-sized white streamer for the white bass, and they'd been hitting it until it was mighty bedraggled. I cast across and let the lure swing around just above the falls, then started weaving in line. Instantly there was a flash, a solid hit, and before I could hit back the fish was in the air.

It had hooked itself and it now went greyhounding up

57

the stream surface, touching water just enough to propel itself through the air again. Its strength was astonishing. Line peeled away. Down came the fish toward the falls now, really streaking. Without any hesitation it shot over the drop, fell into the churning water below, and was gone. I looked in my fish bucket. I had enough white bass for our supper. I quit them right there and went after more golden shad.

That spring we spent a couple of months touring the Tennessee lakes. I kept getting into the skipjacks rather often. I discovered that they would strike small spoons eagerly. But one of the best and most effective lures I used was a small jig. The leadhead jig, born to Southern salt water, was just then becoming a popular lure inland, especially in small sizes, in white or yellow, for crappies. This was a discovery of sorts at the time—jig fishing for crappies. I used them in the fast water below several of the dams, for skipjacks, and found them phenomenally productive.

Fact is, it was a small yellow jig on which I caught my first ones that day on the French Broad. I remember with amusement that I had a date with a local fisherman to go after bass. I became so mesmerized with the skipjacks that I forgot all about it. I even forgot that my wife, Ellen, was roving around the rock fill with a camera. I was just too busy. She was busy, too. I threw all my catch back. She kept hers. The pictures illustrating this chapter are what she got.

6
The Fish That Aren't Afraid

The Gulf of Mexico was a silent, sparkling blue, rippleless and with long gentle swells lifting the little cruiser and then deftly easing it down again in lilting rhythm. We could see no land. We were hunting the wide-open spaces, looking for pelagic species of whatever variety might be foraging here. The skipper was relaxed at the wheel, and I was leaning back against the stanchion of the galley door, with one foot upon the motor housing, keeping a watch behind. There was no hurry. Just being alive and in the vast unpeopled emptiness of the Big Blue was an activity worthwhile in its own right.

But of a sudden I had ceased to revel in it. My attention had been spitted by the stab of an eye staring at me. A large, appraising eye with total naïveté in its expression was measuring the boat and me from no more than ten feet distant.

For one long moment I was utterly awed. I stared back. And then, comprehending, I ran my own gaze over the length and the gracefully streamlined curves of the great game fish that had risen from below to drift beside us, blandly curious and inquiring. It was a sail.

The thought was running through my mind that from its point of view we must present a most puzzling appearance. Just suppose this sailfish had never seen a boat before. Or suppose it had seen boats distantly but had never been stared back at by the eyes of a man aboard one. Regardless of whether or not a fish could think and reason, this must be a startling experience for it, just as it was startling for me.

I said to the skipper, "There's a sailfish beside us. Should we try to take it on?"

But what I was really thinking was that here, somehow, was striking evidence of the vastness of the medium in which the great fish was suspended. It is a rule of nature that the larger a predaceous species, the fewer and usually more scattered its numbers. Here was a species meticulously fitted by nature to its habitat. And yet, as a lone wanderer it might prowl the varied strata of this endless water for its whole lifetime without seeing such a sight as it continued now to appraise.

The skipper looked at the fish and laughed and said, "They can be the damnedest dumb things."

He began to ready a bait for it, but just then it turned slowly as if shaking its head in wonder and drifted on a different tack, leaving us. Here, the sudden thought struck me, was a species rated as one of the world's great game fish—and it was totally unafraid. Not out of bravery. Out of inexperience. Here was a being living in an environment that reeked with fish-eat-fish viciousness, a habitat where violence was not just habit, but *order*. It did not seem to make sense, but I was then hit by the realization that almost all the world's really great game fishes of large size are of the same preposterously naive stripe.

How well I remember as a youngster the group of weedy ponds locally called Five Lakes. Our family had gone there one Saturday for a picnic and to fish. We were in an old rowboat easing along, using cane poles and plunking bait here and there for "roach," as bluegills were colloquially called. There was a sudden flurry of water only a short distance from the boat, and an enormous pike came shooting like a rocket out of the weeds and into the clear. It looked at the boat with what may have been a malevolent stare, or, who knows, perhaps it was only curiosity plastered across a mug cynically shaped by nature into a permanent leer.

Regardless, the fish made no move to leave. In a wild scramble I dove for a makeshift casting outfit on which was a plug my brother and I had whittled. The pike now turned and drifted away, not fleeing but almost as if shrugging the whole thing off as impossible. I hurled the plug after it. The fish swirled violently around. It eyed the plug as I drew it toward the boat. It lunged in pursuit. Whether it actually rammed the boat, I do not now remember. It seemed to me then that it did. Inexpertly, I jerked the lure away too soon. The fish appeared on the far side of the boat and with no backward glance moved on, unconcerned, into the weeds. Here, obviously, was a creature unafraid, juvenile, or stupid. Perhaps it was all three.

What is so intriguing is that all these large game fish that apparently live without knowledge of fear are usually most violent battlers on the hook. I suppose there are many obscure stories untold by big-game anglers about hair-raising experiences with large fish, and especially with the billfishes. One I believe in entirely because I have faith in the authenticity of the narrator has to do with a marlin hung in Mexican waters.

"This fish," the Mexican who hooked it told me, "had already circled our small skiff several times. Because I had caught many of them, I gave it no thought, and put over the bait."

The fish readily took. But when it suddenly felt the hook it made but a single swift run, away. At the end of this one, it turned and came straight for the skiff at top speed and unswerving. If you have ever seen the fin of a big billfish slicing the surface, you can imagine the sensation of seeing it head-on and very close from almost water level.

"I remember the eye of the fish," the fisherman related. "It was very large and glaring straight at us from behind the lancelike bill. Then at the last minute, the brute swerved. I was shaken and I cut the line and started our motor. We looked back and the fish was following for a short distance. I never wanted to catch marlin from a small boat again."

It is simple enough to understand that a skin diver, moving among fish in their element and on a plane with them, may arouse curiosity rather than fear. But, regardless of whether or not danger comes often to large species from the air above, nonetheless this world above the water is to them a forbidden region, strange, mysterious, a never-never land. Just as we, contemplating space, must have our skeptical moments, so even the small minds of big fish it would seem should look above at least with caution. Especially so when man and boat, looming huge on the watery horizon, are near.

Just the other day I watched a hesitant, jittery rainbow trout dart after a bait tumbled through its lair beneath a log. But, drawn out over bright sand as it followed, it fled in high panic at sight of me. Compare this performance with that of a saltwater game fish whose lack of fear is singularly striking—the cobia.

One spring I was off the Texas Gulf coast with a charter

skipper friend of mine. We were talking about cobia as we passed an offshore oil rig. For those who may not know this fish, it is a long, heavy but fairly streamlined brownish-colored species not too distantly related to the fast, fork-tailed group of the mackerels and their cousins. An average cobia will weigh 15 or 20 pounds, a good one will go 30 to 50, and really big ones a good deal heavier than that. The reason we discussed them as we passed the offshore rig is that cobia have a great liking for such places, or for large hunks of drifting debris out in open water.

Ordinarily you do not find cobia in abundance. They are lone wolves, or travel in casual camaraderie two or three in a group. Though not at all rare, they are scattered, and some-what migratory and seasonal. As we talked about them the skipper was putting kingfish lines over for a pair of clients aboard. The morning wore on with much action, and then, when the anglers were pretty well tired out, I happened to look aft and saw something in the water beside the boat.

In the next instant I came jerking upright and was waving my arms and yelling at the skipper. The reason I mention it is that all this time the big fish I had seen, a big cobia, was looking right at me and it was at that moment not more than 8 feet from my waving arms. From somewhere out of the big blue water that bruiser had rolled up beside us. Our prop was barely turning. The fish—which had looked like a possible 50-pounder—was undulating its body just enough to keep even with us. It was almost touching the side of the boat. I believe that by taking two steps aft I could have reached over and patted its broad head.

There is something about an experience like this that gives one a jolt. The fish continued to tag alongside, looking absently up at us—for now everyone aboard was staring back. I could understand that it might somehow mistake a boat for a hunk of drift. But what could it possibly imagine *we* were, and why, with all our wild movement and excited yelling at each other, wasn't it afraid?

The skipper grabbed a rod and a lively shrimp and moved into the aft cockpit. As he dropped the kicking shrimp over he was not a half-dozen feet from the quarry. The bait and small sinker plopped down. The big brown fellow whirled away astern, and just as quickly whirled back. There was a beautiful thick-bodied grace in its movements, and its rich brown, limned against the midnight blue of the utterly clear water, made a breathstopping picture. The cobia slipped ahead without effort, and, teased by the shrimp, looked up at us, opened its mouth, and took the hook.

It dropped back now, and the skipper turned and passed the rod to me. The cobia came around on the other side of the boat. I rammed the hook home hard, several times, making sure it was well set. The fish gave no sign that it un-

Catch of good-sized kingfish, or king mackerel. They, the bonitos, tunas, and the big billfish often act as if they have no knowledge of fear.

derstood. It drifted along beside us. What an eerie feeling! I put on hard pressure. It turned away a bit, moved off. And now, with the rod doubling, for the first time it gave evidence of alarm. The emotion built as it swam away, ever more swiftly, until suddenly with a shocking burst it revved up into a smoking run that took 100 yards without pause.

Above: Even after this big cobia had been on the line a long time, it kept coming back to swim beside the boat. *Below:* Out in the big water schools of kingfish allow boats to pass over or near them, and seem naive about taking the hook.

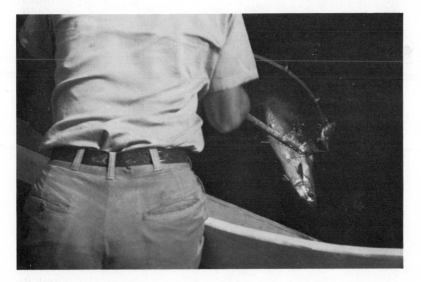

Sometime later—I was beginning to lose track of it—we were conscious of another boat about 200 yards astern. We were drifting now while I labored at the fish. We heard anglers on the other craft shouting. We could see them pointing, and we could see one of them hurriedly readying a rig. Their voices came clear:

"Ling! Ling! Big ling!"

That is a common name for the cobia. Apparently there was a big one by their boat, also. My line was off at a long tangent, but as I worked on my fish I presently realized that the real position of it was in their direction.

Then we heard one of them shout to the fisherman so frenziedly getting his bait ready, "You damn fool—it's already got one line on it!"

It was my cobia. Why, after the experience it had encountered beside our craft, had it been so curious about another? Later it even came up beside us several times, swimming close alongside, although far too green for a gaff. The tackle I was working with was rather light for the job. And the fish was a rough one. It straightened out two gaffs before finally coming aboard—just two hours and ten minutes after it had taken the shrimp! I was not sure at that moment which of us was the more bushed. Indeed, here was a fish unafraid right to the bitter end.

The strange quality of this cobia experience—not an uncommon sort, I'm sure—impressed me. It gave further meaning to the mystery that lurks in the world's big waters, and in the personalities of its big fish. For no sound reason I thought with a shudder of a totally unrelated incident, told at least for full truth by the reputable author of a book in my library.

In African waters there is a species of jewfish known locally as the green chewa. It is similar to huge-mouthed jewfish of Florida waters except that its color differs and its

66

mouth has row upon row of needlelike teeth. Just how large it grows no one can say. African fishermen who should know swear they have seen specimens that will go over 1,500 pounds. There is another difference from the jewfish of American waters. The green chewa is unafraid in a unique manner. It has been known not only to lie and stare at human beings, but to swallow them.

In this instance several fishermen were on the deck of a small craft when the vast hulk of this fish rose from among the weeds and corals and lolled below, its small eyes staring upward. It rose slowly until it was but a couple of feet beneath the surface. On deck there was a flurry of action as everyone crowded around to stare back. An African boy who worked on the boat pushed too close to the deck's edge, lost his balance as the craft gently rolled. With a scream he flailed his arms wildly, clawing for support, and fell over.

Below, the great fish continued to stare, watching the descent, which of course took only a second. But as the jackknifed body neared the water the fish gave a sweep of its tail and eased forward. There was the splash of the boy striking the water. Those who witnessed the awful incident swore that simultaneously the green chewa tilted and threw open its enormous maw. There was a sudden swirl of surface water caused by the suction from within the cavernous mouth. The disturbance blotted out the closing of the trap, but as those aboard stood staring in silent horror, the monster chewa turned slowly and sank back to its depths. There was no sign whatever of the lad.

Sharks are in some respects comparable to that fish. They are among the most feared and least afraid of all sea life. Yet I have often been amazed to watch the antics of the smaller sharks that surely are not intent upon doing any bodily harm to the humans who stare at them and at whom they often stare back. Bob McCarty and I were coming in with his boat one day from offshore on the Texas Gulf coast. We crossed an area where seaweed and plankton had been gathered by currents and wind, and here we saw a sudden churning of the surface. Bob cut the throttle and threw the motor out of gear.

There were several spinner sharks near us, gobbling up small tidbits that lived among the floating debris. As we watched, two of them swimming side by side wallowed within a few feet of us, looked at us insolently, and went on with their work. When he revved up the motor again they gave no sign whatever of being disturbed or concerned.

But when one fishes for sharks of various kinds they are even more unafraid, and insolent. I have watched a 7- or 8-footer come up to a bait put out for it within a few feet of a boat, roll lazily while men stood within sight watching. I have seen such a shark take the bait—perhaps a whole ladyfish—and move along until I could have scratched its back as it brushed past the boat. Even when the hook was rammed into it and it zoomed out to give a hair-raising battle, it never seemed to have any fear whatever.

On Jack Speed's boat out of Port Aransas one morning when things were dull and the water discolored, Jack had his party fishing sharks just for exercise. I got atop the galley where I could look down and shoot photos and I watched a hooked shark come racing up and along beside the boat, eyeing the man who had it tethered as if it were trying to say, "Just come close enough where I can reciprocate and I'll raise hell with you!" And then this same shark, at last breaking the wire leader after an hour on the hook, swung back for a last look at its tormentors. What kind of personality must reside inside the head of such a creature? Certainly a fearless one. Not a lovable one, either.

I believe the most impressive scene I have ever witnessed on salt water was the chilling stalk that a shark—a

14-footer by my estimate—made on a hooked tarpon. There were many people on the long pier that morning. The sun beat down bright and hot and only a minor chop marred the blue surface of the Gulf. At the T-head of the pier a number of enthusiasts were fishing small live mullet for tarpon. One gentleman had hung a fish probably six feet long. A crowd had converged to watch the fight.

I stood at the pier rail watching the platinum-plated tarpon as it leaped and made its strong, swift runs. Then of a sudden I was conscious of a shadow on the water. No—not a

Sharks are of all fish perhaps the most insolent and unafraid.

shadow at all. The form of a huge fish moving without concern for any of us above on the pier, without concern for the shouting and the waving of arms. It was easing almost gently in toward the hard-fighting tarpon.

Someone shouted, "Shark! Shark!"

Then everyone was shouting louder, waving hats, pounding on the pier. To no avail. The shadow there below just moved on, not even hurrying, its malevolent gaze gimleted to the flashing tarpon. And then the tarpon became aware.

It began hurling itself wildly out of the water, forgetting the line now. The shark moved like a lance. When it hit the tarpon there was a sound literally like the smack of a great club striking flesh. Water flew 15 feet high. The tarpon stood on its tail, frantically trying to elude the certainty that stalked it. The shark backed off and lanced in again. I saw at least 6 feet of shark tail and rear portion of its body thrown clear of the water from the jolt of its blow. In the center of the terrible roil, now stained a sudden brownish hue, the tarpon rose again. This time a foot-square chunk of its belly was missing. I felt as if I wanted to look away, yet I, like all the others, was transfixed by the primitive scene.

The man with the rod had been desperately trying to bring the tarpon away from the shark. But on the next lunge of the attacker there was a *pop* and the limp line trailed across the water. The shark had cut it. As the red-brown stain spread across the battleground, the tarpon made leap after leap, each one a bit weaker than the last. And finally the shark whirled away as we all cheered the tarpon and cursed this hated enemy—whirled away and slammed one final blow at its quarry. The long swells with their minor chop rolled on. The red stain spread. Both fish were gone. There was total silence both on the water's surface and above, among us on the pier.

THE FISH THAT AREN'T AFRAID

It seemed to me, reflecting on it, that here was contempt supreme. It is the same kind of feeling I have had while watching a muskie that was watching me. They will often follow a lure close to a boat, flick a glance at the fisherman as if to spit in his eye, and turn away with a sneer of the tail, so slowly do they move off. I have seen barracuda do likewise, only with faster action. Once on the beach at Key West three of us were put atop an old piling by a barracuda and kept there for half an hour. Would it have harmed us? Who knows? I know only two things: who was not afraid, and who was!

But even more interesting than the contemptuousness of those species that are out for no good is the curiously naive attitude of the others—the cobia, the sailfish, the big snook that peers at you from under a mangrove root and continues to peer unconcerned as you cast to him. Or, the stillness of the beautiful, streamlined coveys of kingfish as they glide in blue water and stare back as you watch them while passing above them, trolling for them. This, indeed, is one of the most fascinating angles of the angler's world. Why are the wildest of the big, wild-fighting game fish fashioned without fear?

7
The Dolly Varden:
Who Says They're Trash Trout?

Ever since I can remember knowing that there was such a fish as a Dolly Varden trout, somebody has been knocking it. Sometimes I'd ask one of these knockers, "Have you caught lots of them?" And usually the answer would be either a hedge, meaning they hadn't caught any but were parroting propaganda, or else an admission of failure in trying. Now and then there'd be an affirmative, usually qualified to shave it down to just a few.

I was thinking about this as I stood cranking away at my reel, navel-deep and legs braced with all I had against the powerful sweep of the river's current. It was a crisp and lovely summer dawn on the Middle Fork of Montana's brawling Flathead River, and what I was thinking about mostly was those admissions of failure. After three days of unhinging my shoulder flailing out a big spoon for what natives call "bull trout," it struck me that failure with the darned things wasn't exactly difficult — except physically.

But my fire died hard. There was that first morning. Bill Browning had driven up from his home in Helena to meet me at West Glacier. He had cautioned me that really big bull trout don't get themselves caught by cartloads. You have to patiently whang at them. But when you do hang one in waters like the Flathead, it can go anywhere from 5 pounds on up into the tackle-tearing 20s.

And so, I had for a few minutes made a monkey out of Bill. Dave Thompson, an experienced local angler, was a few paces from me that morning, casting and helping with what instructions he might give me for these home waters of his. Ev Lundgren, who had taken a pair hefting 11 and 14 pounds from this wide, deep run a couple of days before, stood ashore watching and telling me not to get discouraged. I hadn't had time yet. I had made exactly two casts. Ev was simply preparing me. He'd fished bulls for years.

"A really good bull is worth making a million casts for," he said. "And sometimes you have to!"

"Yes," Bill Browning added, "you have to work for 'em."

He said it as I shot out my third cast. I was using a fairly husky spin rod with an open-face southpaw reel and a 12-pound line. The lure was a 4-inch red-and-white Dardevle. It sailed out across the ragged water of the run, came back around with current fighting at it. Just as it straightened, at the division line where agitated water and quieter water met, it stopped.

For a moment I thought, "A damned rock!" You hang a lot in the rocks with these heavy metal lures. Then the rock moved off. It didn't go wild like a big rainbow. Dolly

Vardens don't jump. It simply went away. Not even very fast. Just as if saying, "Why, you boob, I'm a bull from way back and you'll play hob holding *me*!"

Elation roiled around in my gullet. I turned my head and yelled at Bill Browning, "You mean like this?"

Dave Thompson quit fishing and stared. Ev Lundgren muttered that it couldn't be. Then the brute surfaced and rolled around like a bronc snubbed to a breaking post. Water flew. Following that, the bull submerged—a baby sub going down—and just flat went away. It was some minutes of chase-and-hang-on before he began to come home. When he did, I led him toward me, out of the rip of current, into the quiet, and I got the little folding gaff ready, handing it to one of the other fellows, who were sloshing in to help.

Now we all saw the fish. Ev said, "At least 10 or 11 pounds. What a beaut!"

The bull came in as if wholly whipped. He took a skittish look at the array before him. He whirled, rolled, spooning up water with his big tail and hurling it into my face. With power that awed me just a little, he jerked his lip loose from the big hooks. He was gone! I felt, and probably looked, like a tire going down.

To make it far worse, before the morning session was finished I hooked and lost a mate to that one. And so, on this third day with nary a tunk since, I stood cranking and casting and thinking. Everyone else had beached several. That made it more than ever, to me, like Ev said: A good bull was worth a million casts and it looked like I was going to have to make every one.

The Dolly is a handsome fish. In some waters, it is downright beautiful. These from the Flathead were silvery, with pale gold-brown markings along the back, and spots along the sides reminiscent of those on a brook trout but of the palest, daintiest yellow-pink, in some lights barely discernible.

The color, I knew, varied widely within the broad range. I have seen them quite green, shading lighter beneath, and with bright-red spots. Sometimes the fish is called "red-spotted trout." It is, of course, not a *true* trout but a char, like the brook trout, its Eastern relative. The Dolly, the brook, the lake trout, the Arctic char—these are the best-known of that group. The Dolly Varden is native only on the Pacific slope, beginning in a portion of California and running away on up into much of Alaska, its real focal point, and across into and along Asia's northeast coast and on south to Korea and Japan. Inland in North America it reaches greatest population density in British Columbia but is also in good supply in Idaho and Montana.

"Have you ever heard of the Dolly Varden being stocked anywhere?" I asked Bill Browning, who was casting a few yards away.

He admitted he had not. "Nobody wants them," Bill said. "They're supposed to be vile critters, you know."

That's true. Once I went through a whole raft of reference books. These parrot each other, each in turn allowing that the Dolly Varden eats other trout and their spawn and is therefore a vicious thing to have in the water. The ridiculous side is that all trout and chars eat other trout, including their own offspring, and all of them are suckers for spawn, from their own kind and all their relatives.

Bill and I visited about this. "People say bulls aren't much because they'll eat any old thing and so aren't any great shakes as a fly-fisherman's fish," he said.

"Once I found a baby mink in a brown," I said. "A fish that will eat a baby mink *will* eat anything. The most popular bait nowadays in many places for rainbows is cheese."

"And marshmallows," Bill said.

The fact is, all trout and chars will eat just about anything. Dolly Vardens are scoffed at in some quarters because you can catch 'em on a chunk of red meat, or a hunk of fish. Once I caught big brook trout one after the other on chunks of sucker, cut crosswise. I tried chicken guts on rainbows. They loved 'em. The arguments against the Dolly just don't hold up. It has no bad habits others of its tribe lack.

Bill was hung up in the rocks. One of the joys of bull trout fishing in big rocky rivers like the Flathead lies deep in the hearts of the lure makers. They love it, because a fellow has to be prepared to lose at least a couple of lures a day. This can mount up. But if you get cheapskate and careful, you don't get deep enough to catch fish. Big Dollies, like most big trout, stay close to bottom much of the time.

Browning broke off, and since he doesn't cuss, I officiated. He tied on a new spoon. Red-and-white, as usual. For years red-and-white has been a standard killer on Dolly Vardens. On his very first cast, a fish took Bill's spoon, clear off across the swift run, just at the edge of the quieter water on the opposite side. He had out a long line, of course, and when the trout snubbed up and swung into the fast water it peeled line a-sizzling.

"Run, Bill," I said. "Let's see how you can go!"

Bill was sloshing desperately, trying to get into shallower water where he could operate at better speed. He was losing line at an alarming rate. I made for the bank. Easier going there. I ran down through the willows to get below Bill. I had my folding gaff unfolded and was trying not to run it into my leg.

Now Bill had the fish stopped, but it sure wasn't coming to roost. "The books say, Bill, that bull trout aren't very good fighters. Would you give a statement, please?"

"Oh, dry up."

"Thank you. May we quote?" I got into the water and made a swipe at the fish as it argued its way past me. I missed. It looked like maybe 6 or 7 pounds.

Gaffs are popular because so many Dollies here are too big for any net an angler would carry into a stream. But beaching a fish is also good strategy where possible. The shoreline here was well adapted. Before I could make another pass, Bill finally got the Dolly's head up, and ran for the bank. He skidded it up over the stones and then lifted it a bit farther inland by boot. He was panting.

We stood around a bit, admiring the fish. Typically a Dolly Varden is not as short-coupled as the eastern brook trout. It is more elongate. Little ones sometimes look very homely—fish of 12 inches—because they appear so skinny

After many casts any angler is bound to be happy over a trout like this.

toward the tail. But large older specimens become stunningly broad of back, and filled out. They're seldom potbellied, and the weight fools you. It's usually more than you think because they're so muscular.

"I've always thought it odd," I said, "that a fish with such a poor reputation should have such a romantic background surrounding its name."

Several stories go the rounds about this. One is that an English nobleman, enamored of a beauty of his time, gave her name to the fish because of the beauty of its color pattern. Another states that either the fish got its name from a Dickens heroine, or she from it, the Dolly Varden of the novel *Barnaby Rudge*.

She was a lively one, and dressed gaily, presumably like the pattern of the fish. It is said that once after a visit Dickens made to the U.S. there was a fad here of pink-spotted calico dresses, like the pattern worn by the gal in the novel and by the Dolly Varden trout. But there was no romance for this sort of folderol in the hearts and souls of early salmon-canning interests in Alaska, who despised the Dolly, and it was with them, unquestionably, that the propaganda against the Dolly Varden originated.

The fish swarmed there by tens of thousands. They're inclined to be school trout, and, like all the family, when they get a chance to eat spawn, they overdo it. Hordes of Dolly Vardens would follow the salmon runs. Although native peoples in Alaska had long utilized Dolly Vardens for food, everyone agreed that when they gorged on spawn the flesh became soft and unpleasant. Nobody mentioned that this also happens to *any* trout on the same diet.

The salmon canners, however, wanted the Dolly wiped out. It ate salmon fry as well as spawn. The Dolly was so abundant it just plain got everybody mad. At the urging of the canners, it was bountied with Territorial funds. This was

The middle fork of the Flathead River near West Glacier, Montana, is a big stream, with plenty of outsize Dolly Vardens in it.

a little bit like trying to empty the Pacific with a spoon. But the bounty was eagerly accepted by most residents. After all, at 2½ cents each for super-abundant Dolly Varden tails, forty strung on a wire hoop equaled a dollar. These were used at stores and at the poker table just like currency. What blew up the churchhouse was the discovery that a whole lot of other tails—including small salmon!—were getting boun-tied right along with the prolific Dolly.

"I've seen some fishermen shake a Dolly Varden off a hook as if it was some kind of poisonous sculpin," Bill said. "Basically the trouble was that there were, in some parts of

79

I slosh to the bank to beach a good
one.

the range, just too many. They were too easily caught to be considered game."

I snorted and arose. "Maybe so. I guess that's why all these natives around the Flathead like 'em. They're real game — almost nobody *ever* catches one!"

We had fly rods in the car and we walked back along the trail by the river and strung these up. Bill had uncorked a little experimental idea that we wanted to try. He had in a box some of the oddest-looking streamer flies I have ever seen. They were about 4 or 5 inches long and tied in olive, yellow and green. The overall conformation and color was reminiscent of a small yellow perch living in good clear water, where perch often are of a darkish hue, not the bright yellow that they are, for example, around the Great Lakes.

"We know that in some waters out here the Dollies feed habitually on yellow perch," Bill said. "There aren't any in

Above: We hiked in to a wild stretch of the stream to try again.

Left: Dave Thompson, a local expert "bull trout" fisherman, gaffs a prize.

the river that I know of. But we might get the idea cross anyway."

We went back to the stream and waded in. The big flies were hard to cast. It seemed to me our problem was not getting them deep enough. A weighted streamer of this kind, cast with a spin rod, might do it. After a couple of hours of it we gave up. But Bill did know of some big bulls taken on these, and we felt it was a good item to keep in mind.

That night I steaked Bill's fish, which weighed out at 7½ pounds. The flesh was bright orange. My family and I were camped in the edge of Glacier Park and my wife grilled the trout. How anybody could think bull trout poor eating we could not imagine. It was one of the best fish I have ever eaten, very fat and firm and more delicate in flavor than salmon.

We talked a little about trying flies again. I wasn't enthused. It is true that Dolly Vardens are not known as any fly-fisherman's dream. In Alaska in many small waters, where the Dollies are small and chunky, they avidly take dry flies. But the larger trout are used to feeding on bigger stuff and though large streamers readily take them, sometimes trolled as one trolls for big brook trout in Maine, the difficulty always is getting the fly deep enough. In some Alaska and British Columbia locations, where great schools of bull trout swarm in fairly shallow water, of course they'll strike anything at any level, mainly because the competition is so severe.

"In the Flathead and many other places here," Bill said, "they feed on small cutthroats. That's because there is little else available. In some lakes where there are kokanee—the little landlocked form of the sockeye salmon—they greedily lick these up."

It seemed to me that big spoons, just as all old-time bull trout fishermen claim, should be the best bet, and I decided to stick with them. We were back at the river next morning at dawn, getting in where McDonald Creek enters. The water was so clear in the creek it seemed unbelievable. We decided to fish it. But Bill made the error, as it turned out, of fishing from the bridge — just for a few casts, while I started around to go down below into the water. On Bill's second cast, he hung solidly into a good fish.

He fought it like a veteran, but his position was bad. I started to go back up and around, to see if I could gaff it. As I did, the fish went to the other side. The so-called "creek" is a good big river at this point. The situation rapidly deteriorated into total confusion as Bill wore his fish down. By now I was in the wrong position and as I hurried back up toward him, he bent, seized the line and hauled the big trout up hand over hand. He got hold of it as I came in below. I unlimbered my camera to get a picture — and got the prize photo of the trip. The trout gave a mighty flop and plummeted down, with Bill reaching a little foolishly and full of anguish as it fell with a splash and scooted away.

That afternoon we joined up with guide Jerry Messenger, and with small packs we made a walk-in trip to some beautiful water a few miles upstream. Fish had been reported here. The previous day Jerry had floated this wild stretch and had hung and lost a tremendous bull in one special hole. We fished it, and he got into and lost another. Along about dusk, Bill caught a fish, a small one.

"At least it's fun to know you have to throw them back if they are under eighteen inches," Bill said.

That was the law in Montana. I wasn't sure right then that it was fun, however. I'd have settled for a six-incher.

There was something about the next dawn that stirred me. The way you go after these babies is to select a hole and stay with it. I wanted to go back to the hole where I had started, where I had hooked those big ones first thing.

Maybe I could break my jinx. This hole was typical of what the natives call a good "bull hole." Upstream there was a shallows in midstream. Some similar holes will have a gravel island in such a position. Water came racing down over the shallows and immediately below it there was a good slice of midstream rapids. At both edges for at least a hundred yards on down the water was rather deep and slower. But the broad swath in the center remained turbulent and very swift.

"The trout work upstream during late June and on through July," Ev Lundgren had explained. "This movement is actually the beginning of the spawning run. Some hang in a hole for a day or so, some just keep moving right along."

The moment I got into the stream I saw a tremendous trout roll. They do this fairly often, on the surface, sometimes so the entire fish shows. It's doubtful if they are feeding when this occurs. The odd thing is, bull trout experts tell you these fish do not feed at all on the summer upstream run toward the fall spawning grounds at headwaters. This may be true. They are very fat. Every fish we caught we opened, and we never found anything in one.

"In all my years at it," Ev said, "I've never found one with a full belly during this run."

I made hurried casts where the big trout had rolled, but to no avail. Presumably he had moved on up. It's possible each trout you see do this is merely passing through. I cast far across and let the big red-and-white lure swing around. The technique on bulls is fairly simple. Get deep, bump the rocks. Cast across and let it come around. Reel slowly. Try to make the straightening out of the lure come right at the edge of the turbulent water. Most bulls follow this line, staying just in the edge of the easier water but close beside the turbulence.

I was so sure it was going to happen that I was not especially excited when it did. A fish picked up the spoon as if only playing with it. I changed that. I slammed it to him. He didn't seem to mind too much, just turned into the swift run and went away. I went with him.

"Bill," I called. "This is a big one."

Bill reeled up and came along down. Neither of us spoke. The fish fought like a tiger. I kept the pressure on and followed along, giving up every step grudgingly. I don't know how long it took. Finally I had it where I could see it. After that I just sort of fell apart. It was too big to be true. I got the gaff unlimbered and somehow unfolded. Every time Bill offered to help I fended him off. I was sizzling with excitement now and not doing things exactly right.

At my first swipe with the gaff, I missed. On the second I managed to run the point through my wader leg and stick myself so I could feel the blood run.

"The hell with it," I thought.

Bill said a little bit frantically, "You'll fool around and lose *that* fish, if you keep this up."

I got the trout's big head up finally and I sloshed on the double for shore. When he hit the rocks I booted him and there he lay, flopping. I had just landed my first real bull. It weighed in at exactly 12 pounds.

Oddly, this was not the end of the expedition. In fact, Bill Browning had trouble getting me to quit. From then on, for several days, it seemed as if I couldn't get near the river without catching fish. There was just nothing to it at all. I came away convinced that practically everything derogatory that's been said over the years about bull trout is pure bull. There's nothing wrong with the Dolly Varden that close attention with a fishing rod won't cure!

8
How to Be Happy with Walleyes

Most fishing stories start off with line pouring from reel, fish leaping wildly, action, action. This one was different. I had my feet up on a stump and was lounging back on a pile of spruce boughs cut especially for this purpose. There was a line pouring, all right, but it was coming from Bob Blaine's braggety mug.

He was claiming he could make a better Scotch Ram anytime than I could. Since I had invented the drink of said name three rounds earlier from ingredients scrounged from our clutter of gear here in our back-bush fishing camp in Canada, I took exception.

"You just tend your walleye," I said, "and I'll tend the evening bar."

There was indeed a fish, and action of a sort. It had just

done a flip-flop, in the skillet, that is, chunk by chunk, as-sisted and presided over by Blaine. And when I say "chunk by chunk" that is intended to convey that it had been a *big* walleye. Big enough to make a meal for three of us—Blaine, myself and our guide, who thought we were nuts. The wall-eye had weighed, we guessed, maybe 7 pounds. The guide was still a bit disgruntled because after all these years he had learned something. He had wanted us to put a pound of lead on some pool-cue rods and troll down 40 or 50 feet deep to catch big walleyes.

"That is my idea," I had said flatly, "of nothing to do. I'm not that hungry yet."

So Blaine and I, with our guide not speaking to us, had helped paddle around the big lake until we found an inlet, a wild, tumbling stream that pitched down the rocky country, slicing through the spruce and dwarf birch to flatten out as it entered the lake. Upstream only 200 yards, there was, lucky us, a little falls, sharp in its drop-off, and below it a deep, swirling pool.

This was the week of the opening of the walleye season here. It was spring, chilly yet, with occasional snow patches in the deep forest, and the black bears just nicely out of hibernation and fattening on suckers in the creeks and on new grass in the old logging roads. Walleyes are spring spawners. They will spawn in both lakes and streams, but some of those in lakes with a good hard-flowing inlet will sense the current of new water and will move upstream if they can, answering some ancient urge. These could, until they met the falls.

Here, standing on the rocks, using pencil-thin spinning rods and small spoons, we cast *upstream,* let the current roil the lures around on a gently held line and into an eddy, at which time we gave a twitch to the rod tip—and that was all it took. Tip to butt the sporty rods whipped down. There were walleyes in that hole not by the dozen but by the cord. Big ones, small ones, middle-sized ones.

"Are you happy?" I asked Blaine as he went round and round with one.

"Yes," he said. "Are you?"

"I am happy," I said. I looked at John, the Indian who had been unhappy because we did not want to drag deep lead. "Are you happy, John?"

He grinned sheepishly. He shrugged. "When I just sit and you fish, I am happy. I think about walleye in skillet."

There is no better place to think about a walleye. This opaque-eyed, inscrutable fish has been an unflagging gastronomic delight since it and mankind were invented. But for just about that long, too, anglers have been making excuses for it and about it. They are intrigued by it, fish for it incessantly over a vast range, and yet all will admit after the third Scotch Ram, or facsimile, that as a fighting game fish the walleye as usually taken is a cross between a waterlogged boot and a bag of mud.

This, I have long claimed, is because the average walleye fisherman uses his brain about like a bag of mud. The walleye, the next hundred treatises about it you read will tell you, is a fish of clear, cold waters of large lakes and streams that spends most of its time down deep. It is a school fish, and so you wire up a batch of lead and heave it overside and you troll down there, back and forth, back and forth, and presently you hook a walleye. Or have you got one? Well, let's haul up and see. Yes, it is a fish, sure enough. Now you troll back over the same spot and you will hook another from the school and so on until you have a limit. This dull troll-troll chore is excused and passed off as sport on the ground that you have dredged up some awesomely good eating. But as far as sport is truly concerned it is about as much fun as shooting quail tied to a stick.

It is true that walleyes spend a lot of time down deep. It is also true that they spend a lot of time elsewhere, only most anglers still aren't enlightened. A walleye caught in a few feet of water, on civilized tackle, is just as good a fish as any other, and the big ones fight to beat all hell. My thesis is that if you want to be happy with walleyes, break your trolling pole over your knee, melt down the lead for moose loads, and replace brawn with brain. It can become a real love affair.

As an example, in my early angling days I skipped a few grades, sort of jumping from cane pole and bobber (which I still think is a wonderful way to fish) to fly rod. Guys with soft, dark beards may not remember when the first deer-hair bass flies were seen and the first bass fishing done with fly tackle. But us gray, stiff-bearded ones do, and I used to fling such a bug on a long cane pole with salt-and-pepper line because I didn't have a fly-fishing outfit. One evening on a Michigan lake the cussed bug got all soaked up and sank, about dusk, over a gravel bed. I muttered at it and gave a jerk and it didn't come. It swam off. When I got it corralled, there was a 2-pound walleye attached to it.

Some few years later I vividly recalled that experience. It seemed to me that if it was true (which it sure is) that walleyes feed mainly on small forage fish (much of the time about 90 percent of their diet), why *couldn't* they be caught on flies? On sinking flies? And what better method might be pursued than to use a streamer fly, which supposedly mimics a minnow?

How was I going to get a streamer fly sunk down deep enough? I wasn't going to sink it down deep. Even that far back, I had long since discovered that walleyes are not always deep-water fish, that they do come into shallows to feed late in the afternoon and until dusk and after, and also at dawn. A friend and I got on a low bluff overlooking a gravel bar with a weed bed out past it that fell off into deep water. We had a look down there on the bar at night with a light. We learned something.

"Look at that damn batch of fish!" he said as soon as the light struck the placid water. Their eyes all glowed red. In these shallows it was plain to see that they were walleyes. That red eye-glow is a peculiarity of walleyes. But we didn't have long to look, because we learned that when the light hit them they took off. Don't ever forget it.

"Funny," my partner said. "Most fish, like pike or bass, just stay put in a light."

Big walleyes like these spend much of their time in deep water—but not all of it. Knowing where and when they are in shallow water lends more sport.

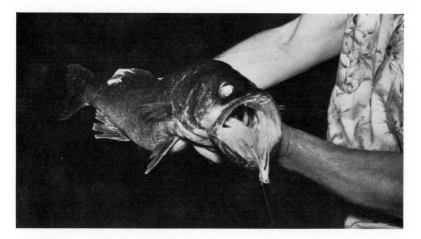

Catching walleys on bass popping bugs sounds unbelievable, but it can be done—and it's much more sport.

A most unusual experience—fishing for walleyes at night with a fly rod during mayfly hatches.

That is true. Still, I wondered how he knew, since night spearing here for those fish was not legal. But I refrained from asking, although I had my suspicions. The next evening just at dusk we got into our boots and with fly rods waded out into the shallows where we could cast to the bar and to the deeper water just past it. I had on a white streamer about 1½ inches long, with some red and tinsel on it.

We were going to be crafty and get set early. Once we were solidly positioned, we moved nary a boot but just stood utterly quiet and waited as dusk drew in. After a bit I heard the slurp of a fish. Maybe a walleye, maybe not. I peeled off and false-cast some line, fishing blind, which was not so very difficult for either of us since we were already experienced at fishing blind at night for brown trout even in those days. Another slurp. Then a rushing splash of a fish chasing a minnow into a corner.

"You hear that?"

At that moment I laid down my fly. "I hear it," I said. The fly sank a bit and I twitched it.

There was an instant strike. A walleye caught this way strikes oddly. It seizes the fly but doesn't race away. I set the hook, of course. The fish started to swim, not crazily at all. And then for the good Lord's sake it just busted out with one wallowing roll and took off on a sizzling tangent. There is no use going into detail about all its gyrations. Suffice it to say that in the next few minutes I learned a lot about walleyes after dark on a shallow bar where they come to corner minnows. They are no bag of mud.

"Beach it," my partner said tensely. "Don't turn any confounded light on."

I beached it. By the time I had fumbled it loose from the fly and cut my hand on its knife-sharp gill cover, he had one. We caught five and then some goof came along and heard somebody there fishing in the dark. He turned a broad-beamed bright flashlight on us and on the water and yelled, "What you guys doing?"

"Fixing to knock your damn head off," my buddy said, reeling up, and straightway heading in to give that very thing a good try. For in a trice every fish had flown the coop.

It is fun to think back to those early experiences. Since that time I have caught a number of walleyes in this manner. Surprisingly, some summer nights when the fish should be way, way down deep are very good indeed. This fishing does not as a rule last long. You have to be there when they move in, and you have to be still. Sometimes a good one on the hook will scare the rest off. It takes a lot of careful experimentation to discover the shallow bars in any lake where they habitually feed. But once you locate such a spot, it usually remains consistently good. It must be a place where many minnows consort. A sparse weed bed on a near-shore bar may be it.

Once I found in Wisconsin purely by accident a bar way out in the middle of a lake where dozens of good walleyes came up at dusk. We had a boat take two of us out there early and drop us off because anchoring the boat was too noisy. These fish are spooky in shallows, just as bonefish or any fish are, even if they are covered by darkness. We'd stand on the bar in a foot of water and cast into three or four feet, and we took a good many fish, all on streamers. Fast-sinking fly lines are great boons to this unique kind of angling. They get a streamer down, in a lake, as much as 10 feet or more in a hurry. One I have has a sinking tip, the first 15 feet. On another, the tip and belly sink but the running line floats. Each can be matched properly to the depth of water in which you are operating. The streamer must be fished *very* slowly. Walleyes are not rash individuals. They just ease up and take hold. Then you must set the hook instantly or they will drop the streamer.

The whole point of these various approaches to happiness with walleyes, I hope I have emphasized strongly enough, is to change them from a "nothing" fighter to a darned good sport. I took a 9-pound, black-backed, golden-sided walleye in a private lake in Wisconsin a few years ago on a dinky spin rod and a small lure, picking it off by plan at dawn from a rockpile that I had found thrusting up to almost surface right out in the middle of the lake. It just tore things apart before I subdued it.

I am not going to tell you all of this is easy. You have to study each hunk of each water. And you have to know a whole lot more about walleyes than most walleye fishermen do. The reason most everybody trolls, trolls, trolls, down deep, with a batch of lead, is that of *course* you can *catch* walleyes that way. It is standard, routine. They *do* spend most of their hours, and months, down deep. But they spend enough hours in shallow water to make it worthwhile and a unique delight pursuing them there with light tackle. Most guides don't fool with it because it is a precarious undertaking. A client might not catch anything. Most average walleye anglers don't fool with it because they're too lazy to think and study and try, too set in their routines to change.

Example as follows. I got wondering some seasons back about that 90 percent minnow diet of walleyes. What about the other 10 percent? I started digging into some scientific papers, reports of studies done here and there on walleyes. In almost all native walleye range, and much to which they have been transplanted, the mayfly (called "fish fly" along the Great Lakes and "willow fly" in the South) hatches by billions each year, this "hatch" being the term used for the metamorphosis of aquatic mayfly nymphs to adult, winged insects. It has long been known to ichthyologists that walleyes are found very often over mud flats.

Why, I wondered? Nymphs live in the mud of mud flats. "Wigglers," as ice fishermen call these nymphs that they use for bait in winter, are gathered by scooping up and sorting mud from such flats. Did the walleyes feed to some extent on those nymphs? I caught three over a mud flat, using the good old spinner-and-worm approach, and their stomachs were stuffed with nymphs. I cast a wet fly with a lightly weighted body, using a sinking line, over the same mud flat. I made it creep over the bottom. Pick, pick. I had a nibbler. I stuck him and boy did he go. I finally wound up a 3-pound walleye that seemed as full of fight as a smallmouth bass.

Later on I got smart and took a tip from the ice fishermen. I tied on an ice fly. For those who aren't acquainted, these are small, weighted flies meant for jigging through a hole in the ice. But I had used them for trout in Western streams and they worked just fine. Here they sank swiftly, and the fast-sinking line chased after. I will not say I had fast fishing. But in two hours I caught three very nice walleyes and they were sporty indeed.

Yet this was only the starter. There was some really amazing stuff yet to come. I was telling a friend about my wet-fly walleye discovery. He said, "Heck, you ever see what happens when a heavy hatch of those great big mayflies is on? They just wallow around, whole schools."

Maybe so. I was not ready to swallow it that easily. Who'd ever heard of that? Then I ran across two scientific papers, one from Iowa and one from a Great Lakes study. Both said, in effect, that when heavy mayfly hatches are on in good walleye waters the fish eat almost nothing else until the hatches are concluded. Wow! Dry-flying for walleyes, I was thinking. Unbelievable! Was there a possibility?

"I accidentally caught a couple," a Minnesota friend told me, "when I was using popping bugs for bass at night. Never thought much about it afterward."

I now reasoned that a cork bug would float much better than a regular big dry fly, which would be hard to handle on a lake. And I doubted a walleye would be very selective. I started watching for hatches. I was visiting that summer with a close friend, the late Red Leekley, one of the most knowledgeable men about fish and fishing that I have ever known. At that time he owned beautiful Belle Lake in Wisconsin, not far from Presque Isle.

Red said, "I kept track of dates on the big hatches for several years and we are about due."

We sat at sundown sipping a drink and gazing out the huge windows overlooking the lake at Red's handsome house. Black ducks paddled past the dock. Then all of a sudden there they were, big mayflies batting by dozens against the glass. I raced for my rod, pressed my son, Mike, into service as oarsman. Out onto the lake we went. Dusk was just nicely closing in.

There were rises galore. I couldn't tell, knowing nothing of this phenomenon, what they were, but they sure weren't panfish, and the lake had very few bass. I had tied on a cork bug with rubber legs. I shot it out among a group of rises, let it lie a moment, then twitched it. Nothing. I started to creep it along the surface.

Gulp!

The sound was like that. I laid back on the light fly rod. Have you ever seen a walleye jump? I have. This one cleared the surface nicely, then wallowed and skittered along the top and plunged down. It took five minutes to subdue the thick-backed brute. I was greatly excited over this discovery. I caught a number of good fish. They were rising everywhere.

I had to leave next day, but I came back the next year. With a local gent I fished the hatches again. He hung one fish that weighed 8 pounds, and if you have ever seen a

96

hassle that was it. Bugging for walleyes, though very specialized and occasional, was, we now knew, a successful approach and a riot of fun and very different fishing.

The whole secret of more happiness with walleyes, I must point out, regardless of the *method* of fishing you use, is to find the fish in shallow water. Fish—any fish—taken deep cannot fight well when brought quickly up to surface. Everyone knows that. It is a matter of fast-changing pressure, plus the fact that to get a hook down deep presupposes the use of weight to an extent that slows down any creature attached to the hook—unless of course you use a "downrigger" (sinker release) technique. Walleyes spend much of the summer in deep water. But they do move out of it in almost all lakes very late and very early in the day, seeking easy pickings in the shallows. Specialized phenomena such as those mayfly hatches, and the nymph-rich mud flats, bring these fish into situations tailor-made for both fly-fishermen and light-tackle spin-fishermen and bait-casters. You can, for example, catch walleyes just below surface on light, small, darting plugs of minnowlike design, or on spinner and worm or spinner and minnow, even when they are after winged mayflies.

In addition, as with all species of fish, water temperature to a great extent controls the boundaries of their environments, both horizontal boundaries and vertical ones. When shoal waters warm in spring a bit after ice goes out, walleyes habitually swarm inshore to spawn and to feed. When these same waters cool in fall, the same shoreward movement or migration occurs. If you will study these periods, and the bottom "terrain" very carefully in your favorite walleye lake, you can catch limits by casting all sorts of light lures with no added weight at all, lures that run down only from 3 to 8 feet. It's just that simple.

The reason most fishermen troll is that they don't think.

Trolling and walleyes have been practically synonymous for ages. So, that's how she goes. What is laughable is that many walleye trollers only *think* they are fishing deep. Make a check sometime on how deep the "deep" trollers *really* get. One time in one of the bays near the St. Marys River in upper Lake Huron I was casting a Flatfish that didn't run deep at all at the slow retrieve I was using. I'd let it sink, then pull a little. I was making potential fillets out of fish after fish.

A troller came past. He said, "It sure is hot fishing, hey?" Then, seeing my stringer and then my gear, "I don't see how you're getting deep enough. I'm taking mine just off bottom."

"Me, too." He cut his motor and looked at me, perplexed. "I know I'm down at least 15 feet. This rig always runs about that at this speed."

I thrust an oar overside and straight down and said not a word. These were seven-foot oars and I had plenty to hang onto above surface.

But forgetting the lakes, probably the most overlooked slice of happiness with walleyes has been for many, many years hidden in the streams. It is curious to me that in northern Canada many visiting anglers catch walleyes by the cwt. out of holes in swift, brawling streams, yet they always come home thinking of this as some sort of phenomenon that won't ever happen again. It could happen lots of times at home if you'd let it.

When I lived at Wolverine, Michigan, there was, I recall, a big hole on the trout-famed Sturgeon River that had for years been called the Walleye Hole. Guess why? On the renowned Manistee, hundreds of big walleyes have been taken. One time I was wading the Sturgeon in Michigan and casting a spoon, with spin tackle, for trout, hoping to take a good one. I discovered a spot that had held several large walleyes possibly for several months. I presume they had come up from Burt Lake during the spawning season, which is when most walleyes are caught in that stream, and had stayed. At any rate, I latched onto a big old brute in the swift water of the Sturgeon and until I got a look (not all rainbows leap) I thought I had a rainbow of at least 5 pounds. I caught my breath after landing this surprise and went right back and got another. Both were, in this clear, swift, cold water, as sporty, stubborn and pugnacious as any trout of like size with which I have ever crossed purposes.

Scores of streams, wadable streams, can furnish this same kind of sport, if you'll let them. Coveys of chilly-

Wading and catching walleyes in streams is perhaps most fun of all.

weather fishermen used to take walleyes at the mouth of the Pigeon River in northern Michigan when I lived there, just as the ice went out. Yet many other streams have year-round populations. I fished the Current in Missouri one year when walleyes to 15 pounds were being taken, just as one would catch smallmouth bass, by drifting and casting into the holes and the pockets. I floated the Manitowish in Wisconsin one summer and shot spoons and diving plugs into deep holes for the same variety of sport, although the fish did not run real large, a couple of pounds on the average.

There is, of course, something about wading and catching walleyes, or floating and doing likewise, that lends angling flavor to this already flavorful and delectable fish. But if you can find on a walleye river spots below the big dams nowadays, or below a falls on a cool, swift stream, you will find walleyes congregating year round, and here, if you will use your brain, you can in due course devise a sporty way to take them.

How? At this time I do not intend, dear friends, to divulge another single walleye secret for un-mudbagging wall-eyes—or for that matter the recipe for a Scotch Ram. But if you get pretty hot at those already noted, well, you will be at least halfway to any further tactics you need. And figuring out the other half—isn't that half the fun of the game?

9
Smallmouth Bass are Different

The close-coupled, yellow-green bass shot out of the water in one of those graceful yet purposeful leaps that are the delight of all anglers. The ripple-broken surface of the swift Northern stream caught light exactly right to mock the action by reflection. Then the fish knifed down into the glass-like clarity of its home water again. I could see it slice away toward the bank, battling hard. I could see the rocks on the bottom, with shadows formed by the broken current sweeping over them.

The bass was no record fish. It was perhaps 2 pounds. But it was a smallmouth bass, and I had hooked it on a streamer fly in cold, brightly rushing water. The situation was so classic, the delight so bountiful—and yet I suddenly wished I wasn't in it. For I had glanced up to see the harassed look on my fishing partner's face.

I was playing host to a young fellow from Florida doing his first Northern fishing, having his first fling at small-mouths.

"There," he'd say in excitement, "is a fishy-looking piece of water."

He would cast his lure into a dead-water eddy, or against a bank heavy with weed growth, or into some area where water turbulence was slight. It so happened that this stream contained, as do many such, both largemouth and smallmouth bass. Invariably, when he hooked a fish, it was a largemouth. He just could not seem to properly appraise the water that would hold the species he wanted.

The day before, when he arrived, I had taken him to a lake not far from where we were fishing now. It contained both smallmouth bass and rainbow trout. It seemed to me this was the simplest way to explain to him what sort of fish a smallmouth is. The lake was deep, clear, cold. Weed growth was only modest, and in no place in matted tangles such as Florida largemouth bass, and in fact largemouth bass anywhere, often utilize. There were sparse reeds here and there, some minor bottom vegetation. The bottom was sandy on the shoals, rocky elsewhere. You could catch a rainbow, or a smallmouth. You never knew which. You could even fish identically for each.

As I played my fish, I said, "Did you see where I hooked him? See that wad of tree roots washed with swift current under the cutbank there? See the big rocks lying deep, with water boiling over them? I got the fly well down and let it swirl in there. When I snugged up and it turned, he banged it. You won't find largemouths in such spots. They're in quieter water, as you've been finding out."

The exasperation of this Southern angler new to small-mouths is unimportant in itself, except as it dramatically emphasizes the difference between our two main basses, and the difficulties potentially in store for the angler who turns from the warm-water bigmouth to that usually smaller but wonderful compact bass with a trout's punch, the small-mouth. My Florida visitor could catch largemouths at home that would make these stream bass look silly, size-wise. But he, like many others, had read much about the steam pent up in the smallmouth's anatomy, and that was what he wanted. His error, like that of most bass anglers, lay in the fact that to him it was simply inconceivable that two bass so closely related could be such totally different fish characters.

I was fishing Dale Hollow in Tennessee one spring when bass were batting lures in right smart fashion. Then we had a sudden spell of really hot weather. About that time two young fellows from Pennsylvania showed up. They fished several days, caught many largemouths. They agonized to me over their plight. Dale Hollow to them had been a long-held dream. Smallmouth bass! Big ones! And here they were, wasting a vacation without realizing their dream. I explained to them that the water they were fishing looked wonderful, and *was* wonderful—the heads of coves, the shoreline shallows, the pockets—for the largemouths they were catching. But those suddenly overwarmed still sections were enough to give a smallmouth a nervous tic.

I said, "If you would seek water not above, say, 60 to 68 degrees, preferably about 65, regardless of what lake or stream, you will find smallmouths at least more *happy* than elsewhere. And most of the time you will find smallmouths, period."

During this same session I watched a very sharp bass angler stand on a rock ledge and cast a lure out only a short distance, then let it clear down to bottom. Bottom was way, way down. He fiddled for a long time, jigging the lure at different levels. Finally at about 25 feet he had a hard hit. From then on it was pitiful. He simply let the lure down like an

Left: Rocky shores rather than dense weed beds usually attract small-mouths. *Right:* A hit along a stand of reeds on a small, deep lake. This bass must have cool, clean water.

anchor. Then he reeled swiftly, bringing it up along the jagged rock ledges as fast as he could make it go. There were many hiding places all down the face of that underwater cliff. The bass, numerous bass, all smallmouths, were hanging around at the same level—a totally different level from the one the less whimsical largemouths were enjoying—and they couldn't bear to let that lure fly by.

Undoubtedly bass fishing would have been much simpler for all of us had ichthyologists named one species a bass and the other something completely different. As it is, the smallmouth has built a reputation as being "smarter" and more difficult to catch than its cousin. And to add to the confusion many a writer cramped for space has written of "bass fishing" as if the two species could be lumped together and consistently caught by the same techniques. Nothing could be more misleading.

The result: We have made something of a mystery fish of the smallmouth, and with no sound reason. It is not smarter. It is not, basically, more difficult to catch. To begin with, it is purely and simply less abundant. Thus fewer anglers build up thorough experience with it. The reason it is less abundant is that the smallmouth bass cannot physically tolerate the latitude of habitat conditions the large-mouth finds suitable. Its range is therefore restricted by its more delicate relation to its environment. It is whimsical from necessity.

In other words, there are only so many streams and lakes clean enough, cold enough the year around, and with proper bottoms and weed growth, or lack of it. Note that the largemouth is found natively literally from Canada to Mexico, while smallmouths were originally almost entirely Northern. There are only so many habitats where temperatures remain constant enough within the limits the fairly delicate smallmouth can tolerate. From all other waters the fish is automatically excluded. Also, the greater share of suitable smallmouth waters are not within our areas of heaviest human population. And so, simply enough, the largemouth, which thrives almost anywhere, teaches the average angler about bass fishing—and when the angler finally gets a whack at the less populous smallmouth he has to learn all over again. Or he should. Many never do.

One of the first things I learned about a smallmouth bass is that a rock is its salvation. Once I was wading a Great Lakes shoreline well known for its smallmouth bass. A point

Smallmouth bass are great jumpers, but not as likely to be caught on the surface as the largemouth. During spawning time a clump of reeds like this often has a bass beside it, on the bottom.

jutted into the big lake. On one side of the point the beach was of small gravel and sand. The other side was of rocks from huge boulder size down to stones about 6 inches in diameter.

Almost invariably, when you find two beaches like these, you can be sure the lake bottom for some distance out will match each beach. I watched anglers working themselves to exhaustion on the gravel side, to no avail. This point, they had heard, was teeming with smallmouth bass. That was true. But apparently the anglers had not checked both sides, then made a choice. Or if so, they had made a most inept one. There was nothing to eat on the gravel side, for there was no cover of any sort.

It did not take an hour to catch a limit on the *rocky* side. One of the reasons the bass were there is that both minnows and crayfish had hiding places among the rocks. The pasture was lush. It should be well noted that in almost all standard smallmouth habitats crayfish abound. And the bass love them. This is one of their favorite foods. To understand about this, begin with the fact that lakes only moderately fertile are rocky and with little vegetation. These are usually the clean, clear, cold lakes, too. Such lakes make perfect habitat for crayfish—and smallmouth bass. The fish have fed on these tiny "freshwater lobsters" for centuries.

Going back to that Great Lakes point, I recall many stretches there where there are shoals of small rocks dropping away to a fairly deep hole perhaps 50 yards across. These deep holes are sandy, but scattered over them are tremendous sunken boulders. You can spot these by their dark underwater shadows. I found if I cast ahead as I waded over the shoals, sometimes in water only a foot deep, I could catch many small bass. If I cast and retrieved slowly over the sandy bottoms of the holes, I could catch nothing. But brother! Just make a cast so the sinking lure dropped atop

Left: Action for a wading fisherman in spring. Bays of the Great Lakes have long been renowned for this fishing. *Right:* A handsome catch from northern Lake Michigan, taken with light spinning tackle.

one of those sunken boulders, and then pull it off! Or cast and work the lure so it crawled bottom under the edge of such a boulder! You were fast instantly to a real fish.

There are, of course, exceptions to all rules, and sometimes smallmouth bass, like other species, are found where one least expects them. But any fisherman planning a vacation of fishing for smallmouths had better select a rocky stream or lake and not bother with exceptions. Or, once on a piece of water that contains both species, he will be most successful with the prize fighter by concentrating on places that have rocks, or current, or both.

I think offhand of a lake not far from where I used to live in the North that had both varieties of bass. This lake also had several highly varied soil deposits along its shoreline. On one side there was a swamp, and here eons of decomposition had laid down a deep bottom bed of black muck from which had sprung a lush growth of lilies and other aquatic plants. This whole shoreline would fairly scream bigmouth at a discerning angler. Directly across the lake a high bluff slanted down, indicating that deep water was fairly close to shore here. There were rock ledges, and the bottom near shore was rather infertile. In some spots no vegetation grew because the slant was too steep, the depth too great. In a few other spots there were slender reeds.

These reeds, well known to all fishermen, invariably grow in much less fertile soils than do water lilies and other heavy aquatic vegetation. In this instance, because boulders were scarce, the reeds made a haven for minnows. And right here along this shore I would always catch smallmouth bass, but very seldom a largemouth. The "reed lesson" can be applied almost anywhere. Such reeds will mean either sand or scattered rock or clay. They will often lead you right to the chunky cold-water bass.

"But regardless of what you say," a friend with whom I was arguing bass recently insisted, "the smallmouth is a great deal more shy than the other."

This is an illusion. Of course you must fish more carefully much of the time for the smallmouth. Not because the fish is more intelligent or shy than its relatives, but because it lives where overhead cover is exceedingly sparse, if indeed there is any, and where the water is gin-clear. In such an environment the fish can see every movement, every shadow, just like a skittish trout. They tend to be more alert and nervous because of this. And often, admittedly, they require finer fishing because large leaders or sloppily fished lures show their faults more in the clear water. Put a largemouth in the same place and it becomes just as difficult.

Sometimes weather can be used to advantage to offset this problem. For example, in a stream that has no great depth anywhere, the swift riffles will be even cooler on a hot day, especially if they happen to be shaded, than the long, deeper runs. If the temperature is not so high that it makes the fish too uncomfortable, so much so that they cease feeding, they will often move into these swift shallow places to take food tumbled down to them. In such a place the broken water racing along breaks up leader shadows also. The same applies when a gusty breeze riffles pool surfaces. If you keep your own shadow off the water near your quarry, and cast carefully, you can clean up.

Mostly you'll do it with sunken lures. It is true that all bass feed on the surface. But the smallmouth feeds so to a lesser extent than does the largemouth. And, since its fare is not so all-inclusive, the most successful smallmouth fishermen are those who stick to sunken minnowlike lures — the streamer flies and the flashing spoons and spinners — to crayfishlike lures fished right on bottom, and to wet flies and nymphs, and small deep-running plugs. Rubber-skirted lures, or pork-rind skirts or pork strip added to a spoon or spinner, all make telling artificials. And, in the bait department, the crayfish, the good old nightcrawler, the small lively minnow and the hellgrammite are the killers.

Of all natural baits, the nightcrawler or its popular plastic counterpart makes the easiest fishing. These are so simple to bumble along an underwater rock wall on the bend of a stream, to crawl snakelike along a rocky bottom, to roll through a riffle. Since they are so deadly, it is often an advantage to fish them rather than other baits, because of the ease of the operation. A big worm is a naturally appealing creature, without help from the fisherman.

However, there are two schools of thought in hooking them. Some anglers hook a nightcrawler just through the head, letting the rest dangle. That's all right, but I have seen times when I fed the bass full without catching one, doing it this way. They'd simply nip off the tails. I discovered some years ago a trick for such days, while fishing in northern Michigan. I used a thin wire hook. I tied a small, close knot to attach it to the limp-nylon leader. I threaded the night-crawler clear on so that the hook point came out near its tail. Thus, the nightcrawler was threaded several inches up the leader. Up there I tied in a very small hook. Its purpose was to keep the bait from slipping down. This system was a beautiful trap, and I invariably hooked my fish at the first nip.

In lake fishing where the water fished is no more than 8 or 10 feet deep, I use no sinker. The crawler is cast with a light spinning rod, allowed to sink naturally, then made to creep slowly over the bottom. Often, if cast against a rock wall, it never gets to bottom before being seized. In a stream, when wading, I have found that fishing the bait *upstream* far outstrips in success the same bait fished down. Here again, no sinker is used. Wading is done slowly, fairly short casts made, the bait allowed to tumble back toward the caster. Line must be taken in at precisely the right speed, to keep snugged but with no pressure.

A very excellent method of bait fishing in a lake, where one must fish rather deep, is to place a bell sinker on the end of the line, and tie a snelled-hook dropper in about a foot up. This rig gets the bait down fast, keeps it just off the bottom, and when fished slowly induces the fish — not so skittish down here in the depths — to follow and hit.

The term "deep," remember, can mean different things to different fishermen. One year in Tennessee I was having a very difficult time of it trying to catch fish. This was in September. That is a hot month in the mid-South. I tried even down to 30 feet, but I just could not find the bass. One day a boat came drifting along and parked about 50 yards out from where I was working away. The man was fishing a wobbling spoon, in silver, as was I. The only difference: as soon as he got located he began catching fish. They were not lunkers, but they were very respectable smallmouth bass.

I couldn't stand it very long. I sheepishly called across to ask him how come. He said, "You're fishing too shallow. Come on out."

I did. I had thought the bottom was even here, but it was not. He was over a hole about 55 to 60 feet deep. I know, many a book says the bass don't stay that deep, that 30 feet is about it. The heck with the books. We caught the bass. It took me back to a summer, when I was a kid, that I caught smallmouth in a bottom-trough in the middle of a lake at about 65 feet, when no one else was catching any. I didn't know any better!

The deep Tennessee fish were caught by fishing the lures just as fast as we could make them go. The gimmick was to cast far, let the lure sink until the line was limp. Then pick up and reel like the devil, thrusting the rod down into the water to make the lure stay deep as long as possible.

This trick, however, doesn't *always* work *everywhere*. In a great many smallmouth waters of the North, a very slow, very deep retrieve gets the big results. You have to keep testing until you hit it. Much depends on how the fish are accustomed to feeding in any particular water. You can never go far wrong fishing the bottom, however, keeping in mind of course the 65-degree temperature rule, too, and acting on it when necessary to come up to mid-depths. On the other side of the picture, during warm weather the smallmouth often simply refuses to hit by day at any depth. Usually this is because the fish is too uncomfortably warm. It is the same as a fisherman eating lightly in hot weather because he feels discomfort from heat and is not hungry.

But, like the fisherman, the fish begins to be conscious of its stomach when evening cools things off. I spent one session in Missouri when I absolutely could not catch a bass during the day. But once the sun had set and the shallows had got cool—at least without direct sun on them—I found I

Fishing the Current River in the Ozarks. Smallmouths are at home in many clear, cold streams.

could take smallmouths even on dry flies, right up under the brush. The reason was simple enough. This rich feeding area had been denied to them during daylight because of its high temperature. Now they could have it.

Temperature actually controls much of smallmouth activity. If I were going to plan a smallmouth fishing vacation, given a normal spring, June and early July would find me fishing waters in the warmer climes, and from mid-June on through July farther north, in Maine, in Ontario, etc. Or, if I could not go then, I would head out in September. I have fished the Upper Peninsula smallmouth streams of Michigan in September and had it all my way, including no crowds—which pull out after Labor Day. I have also fished the Ozarks way along in October and later, and though it is not always as good as in spring, it is often plenty good enough.

One of the considerations in the tackle department I would strongly emphasize for smallmouth bass fishing is *lure color*. Ordinarily I do not place too much stock in the colors of lures making as much difference as many believe. But "color" and "intensity," that is from light to dark, are two very different things invariably confused or at least not separated by anglers. Most persons lump both under "color" and never know it. It may be, for example, that a fish strikes a yellow lure rather than a red one, not because it likes yellow better than red, but because the paler hue – the more intense shade in the scale between very dark and very light – is more appealing, more easily seen, or more natural. In my opinion, smallmouths in almost all situations strike the light shades more readily.

There is good logic here. Invariably smallmouth waters are very clear. In addition, more often than not the sandy or clay or rocky bottoms are fairly light. All life in such habitats tends to take on the paler shades of color, the better to match its surroundings. The minnows are light, the crayfish are pale tan. Thus, lures in yellows and whites, perhaps with dashes of reds – I'm thinking especially of streamer, marabou, bucktail and other flies, rubber-skirted lures or jigs, spinner-and-fly combinations – may appear more natural and appealing to the average smallmouth bass. In cases where the water is stained, or the bottom darker, such as in some of the western Upper Peninsula Michigan smallmouth streams, the lighter-colored lures are probably more easily seen.

Whatever the reasons, in a great many cases I have watched a good fisherman doing more business with yellows, pale greens, yellow-and-red mixtures, yellow and white,

white and red, etc., than with the darker lures. My own experience has been likewise. I have made it a point to use *yellow,* therefore, as the center of my "color scheme" for smallmouths, in a group of varied lures in a special tackle kit. The lures then work out from yellow to paler and darker combinations.

In the flasher lures—the wobblers, spoons, and weighted spinners—one should be sure to have a spread of intensities also. One time when fishing Sturgeon Bay on Lake Michigan I found, oddly, that I absolutely could not catch a bass—and they were swarming inshore—with a silver-finish spinner. I had great confidence in the *type* of lure, and so I switched to a bronze, or brass, finish, and my luck greatly improved.

This was on an exceedingly bright day. Presently I got hung in rocks and lost the spinner. It was the only well-polished brass job of its kind I had. But pawing over my lures, I found a badly tarnished mate. Of course everyone has heard how you must keep all your spoons polished until they shine. And of course this is the worst possible advice. Some should shine, some should not. I tied on the dull spinner, and the bass couldn't get at it fast enough. Undoubtedly the clarity of the water plus the brightness of the sun made too much flash undesirable. In another quite opposite instance, in a swift, cedar-stained Northern stream, the bright silver spoons and spinners were exactly right. The stained (but clear) water made them look a bright brassy shade and the bass ate them up.

There will be times, unquestionably, when smallmouth bass will make exceptions out of all the rules set down here, and out of all the rules ever invented for catching them. But even at those times the sharp fisherman will keep uppermost in mind, in trying to solve his perplexing problem, that this species and its larger-mouthed cousin are two totally different fish characters.

114

10
How Big a Pan Have You Got?

Recently I saw a TV short about that dear, sweet little character, the barefoot boy who fishes with a bent pin and catches a "sunny." This fish, as everyone knows, I'm sure, is in less cozy parlance a sunfish. For decade after decade this overalled kid with the uncut hair has been squishing mud between his dirty toes and soaking his worm on a bent pin. And catching sunnies, which are known in the hugsy-bugsy set as "a boy's first fish."

I don't believe that bent-pin rot. And I don't believe sunfish and all those related and lumped-in varieties commonly heaped together under the meaningless label "panfish" are necessarily just boys' fish at all. It is high time we knocked off this kid nonsense and put the so-called panfish into proper perspective.

As an example, a year or so ago I took a friend fishing

on a backwoods lake I happen to know about in northern Michigan. It contains bass and bluegills. He was a bass addict. It was midsummer and the fish were deep. The first fish he hooked really took the rod tip down.

"Get your line up!" he said with excitement. "I've got an Old Mossback for sure!"

He fought the fish to a frazzle, and should have known long before he saw it that it was a big bluegill. This lake contains bluegills that will consistently weigh a pound, with some 1½ pounds. The average bass here weighs from 1 to 2 pounds, with a few going 3. There is no doubt about it, the 1-pound bluegills fight far better than the 2-pound bass. Fundamentally, they are a better fish, and far superior on the table, too.

"Panfish!" this gentleman scoffed.

About then I hauled in a bass that would have weighed more but didn't do much except wallow around a bit. "If you're talking about fun," I told him, "it all depends on how big a pan you've got."

Who knows what a "panfish" is? Nobody. The species commonly herded into this trap are culled from several fish families. Most are lifted from the sunfish family, which contains all the sunfishes, the crappies, the rock bass and the warmouth bass. Undoubtedly it was this group to which the term "panfish" was first attached. Other species that easily fit whole into a cooking pan have from time to time been tossed in: the yellow perch, the bullheads, the rather obscure Sacramento perch of Nevada and California, the humpheaded, exotic Rio Grande perch of southern Texas and the Mexican border. Yellow bass and white perch have been lumped in occasionally, but neither is very well known nationally. The white bass has been in and out; currently it is considered "game" because of its abundance and popularity in impoundments over much of the U.S. However, if without

Left: This panfish, the Rio Grande perch, is found in the U.S. only in some streams and ponds of southern Texas.

The bluegill, the bream or "brim" of the South, is the best known of all the sunfishes. Fly fishing for bluegills during spawning season is fast sport and furnishes wonderful eating.

fin splitting we treat true sunfish, crappies, warmouth, rock bass, and yellow perch as the important U.S. "panfish," we'll have about all we can handle here. So, let us bend our pins and have at it.

117

Among the true sunfishes, the bluegill is the most popular. It is native to the Great Lakes area and throughout the Mississippi Valley to Florida and Texas, and it has been widely stocked elsewhere. Lakes are its preferred habitat. Bluegills grow to a pound rather commonly, and sometimes larger. Color differs with range, but in general is greenish with darker vertical stripes that fade with age. Males have a reddish or yellow throat, are handsomely blue along the gill cover. The earflap is black, flexible throughout.

Because bluegills are predominantly insect feeders, they're a natural for fly-fishermen. When they're spawning, a surface bug cast into the communal nesting area and twitched gently will really sack 'em up. Because they're exceedingly prolific, it is not harmful to take spawning fish. The males build the nest and guard the young, thus most fish taken when bluegills are "bedding" are males.

Before and after spawning, the fish are scattered out and in deeper water. A few years ago a friend told me, "I've found the killer rig for bluegills—the sinking fly line."

He was correct. I added to it a terminal weapon of a slender-shanked wire hook, with a fly-rod-size pork rind. Often I cut the rind down smaller, or used the tiny white pork tabs now available in stores. This is a prime "wet fly." It is murderous on all varieties of sunfish.

When bluegills are down in 20 or more feet of water, a switch to light spin tackle, with the pork rind as above, plus a small bell sinker, gets the same sensational results.

"Put the pork on a dropper," one addict instructed me, "and use the bell sinker on the end of the line. Creep this rig slowly. On bottom. It works just as well, of course, with a worm or big nightcrawler."

That's true. In fact, full-sized nightcrawlers are better bait for really big bluegills than are small worms. They like a big bite and are vicious strikers. In Florida and Georgia I

118

used to get right out in the middle of a big lake, use a casting or spinning rod and reel, fish the clean bottom by creeping a big worm across it, and mop up on bluegills of preposterous size.

The bluegill is, in fact, best adapted of all the sunfishes so far as sport is concerned, because it can be taken readily by such varied methods: fly-fishing, spinning with small lures, trolling with spinner and fly or spinner and worm, plain old still-fishing, ice fishing. Some of the most memorable sessions of fishing I've ever had—in the South, in the Great Lakes region—have been spent on bluegills.

All of the other sunfishes of a size large enough to allow them sporting stature can be caught by pursuing bluegill techniques. But there are differences, in habitat preference, range, food, that should be noted. Below is a quick, kaleidoscopic view of several of the more important species.

Yellowbreast sunfish. Maximum size 1 pound or a bit more. This and the bluegill and redear grow consistently larger than other species. Greenish, or olive and blue, wavy blue cheek lines, bright yellow throat. Earflap distinctive, very long, narrow, club-shaped. Fish is narrower rearward than the bluegill. Ranges Maine to Florida to Texas to Minnesota, but predominantly of the Carolinas southward and west across Gulf states. Feeds on minnows, crustaceans, insects with little preference. Occasional in lakes, mainly in streams.

"I'll put the yellowbelly up against any fish you got," an old gent in Florida once told me, "and hit'll beat 'em blind for both fightin' and eatin'!"

I've seen many times when I'd agree. However, this sunfish in maximum size can be awfully tricky to catch. In large rivers such as Florida's Suwannee and a host of others throughout the South, it is extremely abundant. Once I

Left: The common sunfish, sometimes called "pumpkinseed," is the one so often associated with the barefoot kid and his bent pin. *Right:* Rock bass are found in hundreds of lakes and slow streams.

caught a specimen that weighed almost 1½ pounds. This one was taken on the meat of a freshwater mussel, a common and excellent bait in the South. Most yellowbreasts are caught on bait. But that's because most local anglers fish them that way. I have caught scores of them on flies, mostly wet, and on small spinning lures.

The common sunfish. Grows to over a pound, but usually smaller. Maine to Florida, throughout Midwest, and to northwest Montana. Widely stocked. Greenish with yellow flecks, throat yellow, cheeks with wavy blue lines. May have vertical dark body bars. Earflap short, stiff, black with long red spot lower rear. Food more from bottom than top, likes muddier, weedy situations more than bluegill, although often found with bluegills. Lakes, also slow streams.

HOW BIG A PAN HAVE YOU GOT?

A few lakes here and there contain really large common sunfish. Although these sunfish take flies, both surface and wet, as well as bluegills do, and can be caught in all ways used for other sunfishes, I don't believe they are as important as their barefoot-boy publicity contends. Because of their food and hangout habits they are seldom quite as good eating as bluegills and yellowbreasts. An interesting note regarding the common sunfish is that I've seen them literally by thousands in certain northwestern (Montana mostly) trout lakes that have weedy, especially reedy, shorelines. In such situations they give fine sport when the trout aren't inclined, and from such waters are delicious. By and large, however, the common sunfish is a kind of incidental with the bluegill.

Redear sunfish (*shellcracker*). From Iowa and northern Indiana to Florida and Texas. Stocked much. Grows large,

Left: The shellcracker or redear sunfish sometimes weighs as much as 2 pounds. *Right:* Especially in spring, crappies by millions load stringers.

in some waters surpassing 2 pounds. Lakes, large streams. Bottom feeder on mollusks, crustaceans, takes some minnows, insects. Crusher teeth in throat. Mottled bluish-green or brassy-green, earflap black with broad scarlet margin at rear.

This sunfish, when you find a lake well stocked with large specimens, is a terrific scrapper and a really sensational game fish. It's greatest drawback, however, is that it is extremely whimsical, difficult to catch except when "bedding." And even then, it sticks so close on bottom and spurns artificials so commonly that it often exasperates fishermen. I've caught a very few on popping bugs, quite a few on deep-sunk wet flies. Ice flies cast with a fly rod also work well because they sink deep, and quickly. These flies are tied with a weighted head and were designed originally for jigging near bottom through a hole in the ice, a popular and deadly method on bluegills in winter in the North. I've adapted these flies to summer fishing and found them excellent. Also, in Texas I have occasionally had fair success with redears by using the pork-rind set-up described earlier for bluegills. Frankly, though, I'm a great believer in "catching fish the way they like to be caught." This means, with shellcrackers, a redworm on bottom.

"I can smell out a big shellcracker bed any old time they're spawnin'," an old Negro guide in Florida once told me.

I believe he could. Many persons claim they can. Many lakes with hordes of big redears give up hardly a fish all year until in spring they gather in great schools in water up to 5 or 6 feet deep, to spawn. Locals usually know which lakes are best. Find one and locate such a concentration of fish—about April in the South—and you'll have the fastest, most fun-packed fishing imaginable. Shellcrackers weighing 1 to 2 pounds—they've been caught much larger than this!—are just plain tremendous for fight, as well as delicious eating.

There are a number of other handsome, sporty little sunfishes. The green sunfish is a widely ranging, much-stocked species, usually found in small waters such as creeks and ponds. The longeared sunfish is a steep-headed, often almost round, beautifully colored species of clear creeks and lakes over much of the South and into Texas. In the waters of Texas' Edwards Plateau they are common, grow to fair size if not overstocked, and eagerly take all sorts of flies and tiny spin lures. The tiny orange-spotted sunfish of the Midwest, a gorgeously colored species, is game enough but too small to be very effective. The spotted sunfish (stumpknocker) is very common in Florida and elsewhere in the South. Numerous other species exist. Where several species of sunfish consort in the same waters, hybrids are fairly common. This adds to confusion for both scientists and anglers. But I feel that fishermen should at least be familiar with the larger, sportier varieties we've touched here.

Rock bass. Lakes and slow streams across middle and northern U.S. Grows to 2 pounds, usually much smaller. A chunky, brassy-brown mottled fish. Mouth large. Eye red, an identifying characteristic. Takes all varieties of food. Often in weedy, mud-bottomed and rocky situations.

Warmouth bass. Close relative of rock bass, but predominantly Southern distribution; Florida through Texas, north across mid-U.S. Grows maximum to a pound, usually much smaller. Large mouth. Dark greenish and brown mottled color. Males sometimes with orange edges on lower fins, and an orange spot at rear base of dorsal. Food habits nonselective. Muddy, or weedy shallows.

123

It's a cinch that anyone who fishes for any or all of the sunfishes will either purposely or inadvertently catch both rock bass and warmouths. Both these species are ready strikers, voracious, and will, like a black bass, eat almost anything, and hit any lure, topwater or deep. Both, as noted, favor weedy, shallow hangouts, neither is as good a fighter as the larger sunfishes, and both are inclined in many habitats to be a bit muddy in flavor and soft of flesh, occasionally also — because of their bailiwick preferences, probably — heavily infested with parasites in the flesh. Nonetheless, they can furnish lots of sport in all sorts of locations where little else may be available. In the southern half of Michigan I used to wade sluggish rivers that had very few sport fishes resident, and have a great time catching big rock bass on flies. At my present (Texas) location, warmouths often save the day when other fish won't hit.

White crappie. Predominantly Southern distribution, Florida to Texas, but also reaches north to Great Lakes. Grows to over 4 pounds, commonly 1 to 2. Silvery with black-green mottlings. Fanlike fins. Large, tender mouth. Body deep and compressed, narrowly keeled below. Dorsal spines usually six, may be five to seven, a distinguishing characteristic. Lakes and large, slow rivers. Abundant in large impoundments. Minnows main diet, takes some insects. Paler in color, and usually larger, than close relative, black crappie.

Black crappie. Ranges natively from New Jersey to Great Lakes south to Texas. Has been widely stocked, now common in Western impoundments. Maximum size to 3 or 4 pounds, averages 1 to 2, but generally smaller than white crappie. Color darker, mottlings heavier and less regular. Dorsal spines generally seven or eight, may be any number from six to ten. Habits and habitats about as for white crappie.

The two species of crappie, though nowhere near as rugged at line's end as the top-echelon sunfish, are unquestionably among the most important fish in the United States. The flesh, though sometimes rather soft, is utterly adored by thousands of crappie addicts.

It is the great number of huge impoundments scattered across the United States and ever increasing nowadays that have made the crappie a truly important fish. They are exceedingly prolific and spawn in locations such as drowned brush and trees, any time from March through June, depending on the latitude. Since impoundments are usually ringed with small willow brush growing in the shallows, or with drowned brush and trees, these huge man-made lakes are virtually perfect hatcheries for crappies by millions.

"If you have access to a lake with lots of crappies but with a clean bottom," a Wisconsin friend told me, "put a big brush pile here or there, held on bottom by rocks. You'll catch a jillion around it."

This man had built, on his own private lake, a dock reaching from shore out to just such a heap of submerged brush. All one had to do was let a small minnow down beside the brush, and take on all the big crappies needed for a meal. In the South and Southwest nowadays, popular fishing docks are furnished with everything down to TV and pop and beer concessions, covered and heated for winter use, and the water around them baited. The bait is usually meal cake such as is fed to livestock. Submerged, it disintegrates and draws minnows, and the minnows draw crappies.

While the great majority of crappie fishermen use minnows and still-fish for them, all the way from Oregon to Michigan to Florida to Texas, the crappie is a darned good sport fish to catch by artificials. Years ago Ted Trueblood tied a fly with a lightly weighted head that was one of the most vicious crappie killers I have ever used. Spin fishermen as much as fifteen years ago were beginning to catch on, in

Tennessee and elsewhere, that small leadhead jigs copied from saltwater jigs, cast to the feet of brush standing in water at impoundment shores, were mop-up rigs. Today this is a standard method of crappie fishing in spring.

It works well anywhere. Not long ago, at a fairly new impoundment in New Mexico, we used a small white jig, fished it in shallow coves around rocks and drowned mesquite, and strung up crappies as fast as we could cast. The lure should be run right along on bottom, and not too swiftly. In Michigan some years ago, my pet crappie lure was a small Flatfish, trolled one oarstroke at a time among stump-filled shallows of a backwater. It was pure murder and lots of fun. But by no means all of the crappie sport is to be had with hard lures, and bait.

For instance, I learned some years back that certain lakes have tremendous hatches of large mayflies at about the same time each summer. When these hatches occur, ordinarily in the early evening, the crappies swarm to surface. Panfish fly-fishermen should be aware that most of the true sunfishes stop feeding by full dark or shortly after, but crappies are great night feeders. With bushy dry flies, and a flat lake surface, one can catch good strings during the hatches. On occasion crappies will hit modest-sized popping bugs, too. It is confusing and unfortunate, but undoubtedly a mark of panfish popularity, that every one of the species in this category has been given local names by the dozen. The sunfishes have gathered in long lists of colloquial names. Once I made up a list of over fifty names attached to the crappie.

As an example, a man in Tennessee told me one fall, "The newlight have been bitin' right smart in the river."

He meant crappie, but another Southerner explained to me that newlight were really papermouth perch. And a papermouth perch was the same fish as a tin perch. This was certainly different from a robin perch, the name given the yellowbreast sunfish by another fisherman I met in South Carolina. In Texas everything that isn't a bass is a "l'il ole perch." I have seen cane-polers with several species on a stringer who did not even recognize that the various fish differed from each other. All were just "perch." The *true* perch is of course a quite different fish.

Yellow perch. Same family as walleye and sauger. Natively and by introduction ranges from eastern Canada to the Pacific, south to the Carolinas and west across entire mid and northern U.S. Grows to over 4 pounds, commonly to 1 pound, but averages less. Body elongate, dorsal fin with two separate portions, spined, and soft. Color greenish-bronze on back, shading to yellow on sides, with distinct dark vertical bars. Main diet, minnows, but takes variety of food. Mainly in lakes, some in slow rivers.

"I don't think the yellow perch is really a game fish," an old fishing friend of mine in Michigan used to say. "It's an *eating* fish."

The description is apt. In many places, especially the Great Lakes, the yellow perch has been a big-time commercial fish ever since early settlement days. Actually, though yellow perch are fun to catch, they really aren't much as

Yellow perch are among the most abundant and delicious of the so-called panfish.

fighters. And, though they will take artificial lures, from flies to small plugs to spinners and spoons, minnows — and occasionally worms — are the real perch catchers. The only difficult part of catching perch is locating a school. Once you find it, they're invariably ready. In very early spring, perch "run," crowding into slow streams and dredge ditches and bayous and bays adjacent to big-lake waters, to spawn. I've fished them around the Great Lakes shores when one could catch hundreds as fast as bait could be put down. After spawning, they go into deeper water. Once in a North Dakota lake I caught a big bucketful of 12-inchers by fishing on bottom in 25 feet of water, with crawdad tails. Ice fishermen catch yellow perch by millions, too.

Fun, yes. But it is the eating one looks forward to. I can't recall who was responsible for the quote, but I remember it from some book — to the effect that the single fish one could eat day after day and never tire of is yellow perch. And this awakens one of the fondest of my fishing memories. . . .

The time was fall, the place the northern Lake Huron shore out toward Cedarville, Michigan, where numerous islands — Les Cheneaux — dot the protected waters of this ragged shoreline. We weren't actually on a fishing trip. Oh, no, not when fall had painted the maples and the birches. We were after ruffed grouse. And ducks.

Talk about busy! We'd walk the steep rises and the heavily timbered slopes of the shore, listening for that wonderful thrill of Old Ruff rising in an explosion of winged sound to startle the calmest shooter. By mid-morning we'd be in, bushed to the sox, and if we'd shot well, which is to say hit every fourth or fifth bird up, we'd have limits to clean. But there was no time to waste. Immediately after lunch, into the boats we'd fall, and with decoys heaped high we'd head across an open stretch to a likely point where the bluebills, or the mallards and blacks, would surely stool toward evening.

In the midst of the heaped duffle, underneath it all, in each boat was a washtub, an empty washtub. And stowed up front were some short fishing rods. Once the decoys were set, away we'd go to those great old spots we knew of, where the perch lay corded up down below and were big and fat and always hungry. On many a crisp afternoon I've seen those tubs fill up fast. There was a limit, as I recall, 25 or 50, I forget which. But the perch were big and with three or four of us to a big boat we poured the pounds of flopping fish in. Then a straggling line of ducks would whisk over, cutting high and then slicing down toward our decoys, and right there the perch fishing ended.

It ended, that is, until we crawled in exhaustion up the slope to the cottages where we always stayed, lugging our ducks and our tubfuls of perch. Then we'd gather around the big table, and the woman who took such good care of us each fall, and whose husband hunted and fished with us, would bring out platters heaped with scores of fried perch, all skinned and boned in a unique way she had of doing it. Good? Friend, they were downright awesome.

Funny, I don't even remember the awful agony of cleaning ducks, stone dead tired, while this fine couple cleaned and froze big packages of yellow perch for us to take home. All that is bright in memory is the fun. And then I skip back fish by fish, species by species over the years, and it is a curious thing. There aren't very many big fish I remember, nor so very many huge, indescribable thrills. But there are untold times recalled of furious action hour after hour with small fish—panfish, I guess they are. It all depends, as I've said, on how big a pan you've got. Fishing is supposedly for fun. Small fish lumped together as panfish have given me much. Lo, my pan is large, and overfloweth.

11
Mining Bass in Kansas

There was no question about the size of the bass. Bud Coons laid the popping plug nicely alongside the bank and the critter took it with a sound so big I was sure we'd have to hang him by a rope from a willow limb to gut him. That is, if Bud won the fight.

The neck of water was slender, the bank steep. Bud tried to follow as the bass charged down it. His off foot kept slipping into the water and at every step he talked to the bass in brittle language.

"Do they always run that way?" I said, watching.

"No," Bud answered with biting sarcasm. "Sometimes they run the other way." The fish, apparently hearing, swapped ends and came toward me.

I could see it in the clear water from my vantage point atop the ridge. It was shoat size and giving all it had. I saw it nose upward, break the surface. It jumped ponderously and fell back with a rousing splash.

Across the slim waterhole, one of Bud's foremen from his recreational vehicle factory in Oswego, Kansas, stood watching. Bud had invited several of his men out for this shindig. At the man's feet, on a stringer, were several bass of a size that had given him comparable brawls. He cried, "Bud, don't lose it. It'll go 7 or 8 pounds!"

This was the wrong thing to say. The bass plunged upward once more. The plug sailed ashore and hit with a splatt in the grass. The big fish fell into the hole it had opened in the surface, and disappeared.

I stood up. Purposely trying not to witness Bud's disappointment and chagrin, I looked off over the endless undulations, the narrow slits of blue water between the sharp ridges of grass-grown earth. I had come here to the southeastern corner of Kansas full of doubt and disbelief. I had come expecting to see a horrible mess of countryside rent and ruined by man, a mess in which by some miracle a few puny fish had been able to survive. Instead I had found what is among the most unusual and best largemouth black bass fishing in the United States.

It is quite a story—for several reasons. First of all, fishermen don't exactly swarm to Kansas. I asked a fellow once if he had ever heard of the strip pits in southeast Kansas and he said, "No, I never even heard of Kansas. Can you drive to it?"

The fact is, of course, that every state has at least some fishing, and if you are a native in Kansas and know the various waters you do get good fishing. But the state has never been known nationally as any paradise for visiting anglers, has drawn few, and is no water wonderland. All of which just goes to show that there is always something left to be learned. Because *this* corner of Kansas *is* a true hotspot,

131

and *this* corner *is* in its unique way a water wonderland.

The second reason was evident when we walked along the ridge to the next long hole of water. Bud was carrying a stringer with three bass on it, and as we authenticated later, that trio weighed in the aggregate a few ounces over 20 pounds!

He stopped suddenly. "Stand real still. Look down in that hole below us."

I did. I saw a bass fanning lazily along. It had not yet become aware of us up above. It reminded me of the old joke about the guy who said he caught a 12-incher — 12 inches between the eyes. Suffice it to say that it was larger than any Bud had on his stringer. We let it pass, then crept down to water's edge and Bud made a few casts. Nothing doing. We had probably spooked it.

No matter. The point is, these oddball waters are choked with bass like that, as well as with smaller ones. Just why these pits should grow such good fish is not easily explained. As I've said, I had expected to see a horrible mess of landscape here and to listen to the populace moaning about the dastardly deeds of the strip-mine people. That gets us to the third reason why southeast Kansas is quite a story.

Surface-type coal mining has been going on in this region for a long, long time. In the early settlement days coal was discovered, was laboriously dug, and traded to some extent. In later years, as strip mining was developed with its ponderous machines that gouge the earth off the top and the coal from beneath by digging trench after huge trench, the flat region was slit to pieces.

All of us have read, I'm sure, the articles raging at the disgraceful practice of strip mining. I saw one not long ago that led me to believe that at least in certain portions of the East the end of all water resources, fish, game, and perhaps even the world itself was at hand because of the desecrations of the strip miners. That may be. There. But as I stood here watching Bud Coons now lay cast after cast up along the bank of a pond that was only one of thousands in the surrounding region, I reflected that surely there is no argument on earth that doesn't have two sides.

At that moment, Bud's foreman, up the neck of water from us, let out a whoop. We turned. A bass shot out of the water and went hopping over the surface.

Bud said, "Look at that crazy devil go!"

His own popping plug lay inert as he said it. There was a hell of a splash. We jerked our heads around. Bud automatically reefed back on the rod. He was fast to a good one and it took off down the slice of deep blue water, scattering a covey of bluegills or crappie or some smaller fish as it plunged like a bucking bronc, throwing water all the way.

Here, indeed, was the other side of the argument. Strip mining, to be sure, does raise hob with the landscape. The giant shovels—the second largest in the world has operated in this area—stalk across the countryside foot by foot like nether-world monsters. An enormous trench is scooped out, with the residue piled in a ridge. Next to that ridge another deep trench is dug, and another ridge formed. Where a big deposit is found, larger potholes may be gouged out, or wider, deeper trenches. A piece of country freshly worked by the strippers is as sorry a sight as can be seen—grassless, treeless, a no man's land of mud, slag and seepage water, with hellish barren undulations anguishing across the jumble.

As the various articles have stated, acids then become a problem. The soil won't grow certain plants. Sometimes none will grow. The first water to seep in is not habitable by any aquatic life. But now old Ma Nature begins to knead the whole mess and fiddle with it. Slowly, slowly the soil "weathers," the water clears, the trenches fill. In places well drained by streams, run-off damage may be severe. But again, Kansas is the other side of the argument; few streams are here.

Mining companies, well aware of the stigma attached to their acts, have for years now been active in rehabilitation of some of their stripped areas. They deserve credit at least in those cases. They hire agronomists, foresters, fisheries men, game men. When a newly decimated hunk has "weathered" long enough, tests are made to see what will grow. Grasses are sown. Trees are planted. Fish are stocked.

Bud brought his bass onto the bank and put it on his stringer. I said, "What water was there around here originally?"

He replied, "The Neosho River, a few small lakes, mostly man-made. Not much, really."

"How much public water is there now? Strip-pit water."

"Lord," he said. "Lots. It's difficult to figure exact water-surface area. There must be 10,000 acres of strip land right around here that is now reclaimed for recreational purposes. And the ponds and channels number in hundreds."

"Do local people despise the mine people?"

Bud was incredulous. "Hell, no! Most of the mines open rehabilitated pits to public fishing and hunting. Sportsmen's clubs develop other chunks. The state has been buying others and now has a lot that're wide open to anybody, local or visitor. The strip mines have actually changed southeast Kansas from a near-fishless region to a fisherman's bonanza, and we get wonderful duck hunting, too. We desperately need this recreational land and water. We were a 'have-not' and now we're a 'have.' "

Bud's estimates, I discovered later, were low. To give you an idea of the opportunity awaiting a visiting fisherman here, Crawford and Cherokee counties in the southeast corner of Kansas have over 50,000 acres of pit lands. Of this, at least 12,000 acres is water anywhere from 6 to 50 feet deep. Early in the rehabilitation process two sportsmen's clubs in particular were extremely active in developing pits. The Cherokee County Sportsman's Association charged a low annual membership fee, and developed a large acreage, with boat-launching facilities at the larger pits, and camping and picnic installations. They even established rearing ponds where they raised fish to stock some of the pits they were supervising. The Sunflower Sportsmen's Club east of Parsons did much the same.

But the big deal in southeast Kansas nowadays is the pit land the state has purchased and developed. Shortly before I fished the pits a new 2,300 acres were purchased near West Mineral. This was soon under concentrated development. Other pit land, in the same general region, already owned by the state at the time ran the total to at least 6,000 acres, and the state was shooting for development of at least 10,000 acres. A sizable part of this was reachable during my visit on blacktopped roads, by going a few miles east and north out of Oswego, Kansas.

Bud and I took a drive around some of this during the afternoon. It was a revelation. Access was easy to all the general areas of pits. Twenty-odd miles of new access roads had recently been built through the pit sections, and some 60 miles of foot trails were cleared and marked. We counted twenty-seven parking lots, numerous tables and camp shelters, and many double-unit rest rooms. I was introduced to Gene Wright, a state man who was then permanently stationed on a several-thousand-acre pit recreational development near Columbus, Kansas.

Gene said, lifting the lid on Bud's ice chest and looking at bass we were taking to town, "I guess I don't have to tell you that the bass fishing is great. But we also hope to make a real humdinger hunting area out of this. Ducks, deer, quail, pheasants. It'll be just about a year-round paradise for

135

sportsmen. They can come here to do anything they wish, and camp right on the grounds."

I asked him if he had any dope on record catches out of the pits. "Well, I don't know if they're records, except maybe around here. But I can tell you that nobody gets overly excited over a 7- or 8-pound bass. One fisherman near West Mineral has taken twenty bass so far this year that bettered 8 pounds. Used minnows. We had one bluegill turned in that went 2 pounds 2 ounces, a crappie of 3 pounds 4 ounces. Some good walleyes are now showing up—they were stocked experimentally several years ago. And of course channel cat are an everyday occurrence."

On the way back to our fishing spot, Bud told me that it was expected the pits would constantly increase in the area for some years. The beauty of this water is simply that there is no single enormous body of it to bumble around in. You can learn one pit at a time. And there's always another one to discover. You could fish a new one every day for a lifetime!

He drove past where "The Brute," as it is sometimes called in the region, was at work. This is an awesome strip shovel operated by the Pittsburgh & Midway Mining Co., near Hallowell. It bites off 95 cubic yards of earth at one scoop! It could, I reflected, pick up our car and dump us without even knowing we were in its load.

When we got back to "camp," some of Bud's boys from the shop had a big lunch going. This was one of the oddest camps I've ever fished out of, and one of the most pleasant and elegant. The pickup coach, as everyone knows nowadays, slips into a pickup truck and thus becomes a kind of wheelless sports trailer. But Bud's company had fixed up a unique rig by which a pickup camper was turned almost by magic, since little elbow grease was involved, into a houseboat.

136

We parked and walked down to where one of the units we'd been using was moored. We had three of them on this scattering of large pits today. I stepped out on a pontoon and went aboard. The outfit consisted of a set of big pontoons on which a deck was secured. The sides of the deck could be folded up, so it and its pontoons might be towed on the highway on a special trailer built purposely to haul it. The coach meanwhile would ride on the pickup.

We had put one of these in the water this morning. The operation consisted of unfastening the coach, slipping special jacks under it. Then, driving the pickup gently out from under it, we simultaneously hauled the pontooned deck beneath it, let it down, secured it to the deck, and backed the whole shebang into the water. Presto — a full-fledged houseboat! At the rear was a motor bracket that raised and lowered. Up front under the shade of the overcab bunk was the wheel and gear shift.

Bud plumped into a chair by the controls now, started the motor. "Cast her off," he said.

We slipped the rope and he ran down a long, blue channel and came to rest beneath some overhanging willows. We hit the lunch like a scourge of locusts. The boys had fixed it, of course, on the stove in the coach — or houseboat — and we had ice-cold beer from the ice box, drinking water from the tank and pump inside, fine beds to recline on, or a table to lounge at if we chose.

Presently some of the others Bud had invited came chugging past in another unit similar to ours. They were towing a skiff. One of them was in it. Those aboard cut the boat loose. The occupant made a cast, promptly hung into a bass of at least 3 pounds, and wrassled it to a finish. He moved the boat over close to exhibit his prize. Somebody yelped. I looked up to see the other pontooned coach now parked in a cove. One of the guys was at the back, and he

137

had a bass on. I grabbed a camera. The bass sailed out of the water obligingly. Crazy, I thought. Here I am in dried-up, unpublicized Kansas of all places, surrounded by water and houseboats and bass. It didn't make sense.

"Did I tell you," Bud interrupted my thoughts, handing me a fresh and frigid beer, "that one of the guys on that boat took a bass while we were gone that weighed *9 pounds?*"

We lazily put in the hotter part of the afternoon, moving whenever shade left us, and occasionally taking a swim. The waters of almost all the pits are cool and exceedingly clear. Presently we heard the insistent honk of an auto horn, and Bud turned the boat back toward where we had launched. A car with official insignia was there. I was introduced to Tommie Crispino, the local warden.

Crispino knows as much about catching bass in the pits as anyone in the entire region. He has fished scores of them, has caught an enormous number of bull-sized bass.

"What's your favorite weapon for these bass, Tom?" I asked.

He grinned. "A camouflage suit."

It's true, Bud assured me. When one fishes from the bank here techniques become rather specialized. For in order to get to any pit you have to walk a ridge, or cross a ridge, or come down off a ridge. These banks are exceedingly steep. This puts the fisherman in a position of looking down on his potential fishing water. He is easily spotted by fish from below in the clear water. His shadow is easily thrown upon a narrow, deep neck that may contain a bruiser.

"I like an overcast day," Crispino said. "I — well, heck let me show you."

He got his fishing rig out of the car, slipped on his camouflage suit, and came aboard. We took him up to a spot where he could operate in the lengthening shadow from a ridge.

Far left: The huge strip-mining shovel scars the landscape. To get an idea of its size, consider the rutted roads made by trucks. *Left:* The beginning of rejuvenation, with water everywhere. *Above:* Pickup coach secured to pontoons and deck moves along one of the larger strip-mine pits.

139

Climbing it, with Bud and me lagging behind to watch his technique, he said, "If you want to consistently catch big bass here, day in and out, you have to think of this more as hunting than as fishing."

On hands and knees he eased gently over the top. We crawled up and watched. In slow motion he moved down toward the water, blending perfectly with his background. He had explained that no jarring footsteps should disturb the quarry. He could not have set up a more convincing demonstration, for as we watched we saw a fine bass cruise along within feet of Tommie. He hunched, frozen. He had a big plastic worm on his spin rig. When at last the bass, still unaware, was out of sight, he flipped a sidewinder cast, keeping the rod near water level and barely moving its tip with a quick flick of his wrist.

The lure shot well over to the far side. If the bass had kept going, it had by now turned to cruise back along the far bank. We could not, of course, be positive it was the same bass. But we saw Crispino's rod tip jiggle, then bend snugly. He eased off line temporarily, letting the old geezer munch the fake worm. Then he let him have it.

Wow! The rod whipped forward. There was a wild roil of water. Then a massive splash. I wondered in a whisper why Crispino didn't stand up.

Bud said, "He figures he'll land that one and creep right on down the bank after another."

But he didn't land it. The bass somehow shed the hook and streaked away. From where we peeked over the top we could see it go. Crispino hardly turned his head. He eased on along, squatted, waited maybe five minutes, made another cast. Nothing. Another cast. And, this time, he hit one like a chunk of concrete. It took line and then sat up atop the water on its haunches and flippered its way with noisy splashing for what seemed like half a mile.

"That louses it," Crispino muttered. He arose and gave the bass a hard working over and presently brought it to heel. He turned it loose, came up the bank grinning. "I was lucky," he said. "But anyway, that's how you do it most consistently."

Crispino finds big minnows excellent here. But you have to steal down to the bank and stay sitting, close to the water, making no fast moves and in fact as few moves as possible. Patience is the word. The minnows he fishes down around 6 feet most of the time. He uses crayfish, too. Light-colored ones are best, he claims. Easy to see. The smaller ones take some huge bluegills. Early and late, at proper seasons, he also fishes topwater lures, as we had been doing. He thinks however that, all told, deep-working lures most consistently take a big fish.

"If you don't have camouflage clothing," he told me, "be sure to wear something dark. It helps." We had not done this, and had caught fish. I have no doubt nonetheless that Crispino's ideas are best in the long run. We had probably spooked far more than we'd caught.

On a fairly recent visit to the strip-pit region, I discovered that fishing was still just as good as ever, but that the mining operation had been closed down. The entire business had been sold, the huge shovel and all the workmen moved out. The new owners of this enormous project felt it was no longer profitable to strip-mine coal here. However, during some of the final digging, "The Brute" had stalked over some already stripped areas and scooped out holes as much as 60 feet deep. Thousands of acres were still open to the public, and as the years go on, it is believed, fishing, and the look of the land, will become progressively better than ever.

That first trip using Bud's interesting and comfortable little crossbred houseboats, however, unearthed fishing that couldn't get *much* better. After the session watching Crispino, we put in the late afternoon and evening fishing the lazy way, drifting or easing the houseboat along and standing on deck shooting a lure out ahead or to the bank on either side. We caught bass. We failed to take anything big. Perhaps it was because we were somewhat sated with it. The evening was so enjoyable it was too easy to relax and fish with little purpose. One of the boys skinned and filleted several of the big bass and Bud set up a charcoal grill on deck and broiled them. With a Scotch or two to whet appetites, we shortly found ourselves too full to wiggle. All hands turned in. It was a gentle thing indeed, sleeping aboard to the minor sway of the pontoons as a breeze ruffled the surface.

But my wonderful reveries were shattered when Bud jabbed me in the ribs at daylight. "Up," he commanded. "We're wasting the best part of the day."

"This?" I gasped. "This is *day?*"

He baited me with coffee, prodded me ashore. We got into his car. He burned up the road for a short run. Groping in predawn light, he led me to the bank of a dark, deep hole of water.

"Cast there," he ordered.

"Where am I?"

"Well," he said, "this is one of the sportsmen's club spots that I have watched a long time. I have seen bass cruising in here that — well — there's no use telling you — you wouldn't believe it."

I raised the rod. I saw a wake I took to be caused by a swimming muskrat. Then my hair went up. A fin was showing in the forefront of the V. I let the lure, a surface chugger, fly. I brought it back crossing in front of the V. I do not wish to try to describe what happened. I'm not sure I know precisely. I thought first I had scared hell out of something. In the next second I knew that was wrong. It had scared hell out of me. It didn't strike. It engulfed. There was a sucking, gurgling sound, but amplified until it wasn't sporty, or thrilling. It was unbelievable. Then the thing just simply went.

Line went. Rod went, tip down to the water. I went. "Bud!" I yelled. "Bud! I believe it! I've *got* it!"

I think Bud said something. Or tried. The bass jumped. It was too big and fat to really jump. More properly, it floundered, showing itself momentarily. But when I laid back on the rod, I began to fall backward. There was nothing to brace against. The bass was gone.

At daybreak I am not ever in tune. My level of capacity for the general shocks of living, like moving around, or making sense out of what people say such as "Good morning," is at roughly moccasin height. I sat down. I quivered.

Bud said, "Do you have retractable stalks for your eyeballs? If so, pull 'em in and we'll catch another. There are more."

"Bud," I replied weakly, "I am not a morning drinker. But I seem to recall there was a dollop of Old Panther dregs in that bottle from last evening. De-rig this damned rod and take me to it, will you?"

Author wades, and jumps a big one. These waters are now clear and fish-filled, and open to the public.

143

12
A Plug for Trout Plugging

For centuries, trout have been identified with tackle suitable for casting flies, purely because of tradition. That tradition is still strong. Until the immensely successful invasion of the plug man's domain by the fly-fisherman, and later the introduction of spinning to the United States, the users of artificials were split into two camps. You were either a fly man, which meant trout fisherman, or you were a plug man, which meant bass and pike. A great many, of course, were double-threat men.

The strange part is that over recent years, while fly-fishing was spreading out to include every conceivable species, nobody thought much about making the reverse switch: bass tackle for trout. To assume that big trout would turn down big lures, just because their general food was small, and small lures traditional, is not very imaginative.

I remember an instance that made quite an impression on me. I was fishing the Manistee River in Michigan, and a friend of mine picked up an awesome old brown trout, floating belly up, apparently dead of old age. I believe that trout would have weighed 15 pounds, possibly more. It had probably seen thousands of flies cast over it, but hadn't fallen for them, at least not fatally. We opened its stomach. It had fed well prior to turning up its fins. In it were two frogs, an outsize crayfish — and a baby muskrat! Suppose that somebody had heaved a bass plug at this trout, a contraption it had probably never seen before. Possibly today it would be hanging on that angler's wall.

I have seen some curious items come out of the gullets of big brown and rainbow trout. Frogs are extremely common. So are crayfish, some of them practically lobster-size. Huge hawk moths, mice and birds turn up regularly. I have removed snakes from several. Trout and suckers of 8 or 9 inches are extremely common in the stomachs of lunker browns and rainbows. Even a baby mink has been found in a big trout! A fish that would gobble a mink isn't very choosy.

In other words, when a trout reaches maximum size and is in its prime, especially when it has ceased to feed much on the surface, it is a most voracious critter — a killer, a glutton. It doesn't eat off-trail dishes every day, to be sure. It doesn't get the chance. But when they do appear, often as not the trout grabs 'em. By the same token, it doesn't see bass plugs every day. When it does, there's a fair chance, if the presentation is lifelike, that the fish will take a smash at one.

One year I made a float trip on the Paint River, a tremendously wild, big river in Michigan's western Upper Peninsula. I was after smallmouth bass, but because of high water I wasn't doing much. Mike Strengberg, a forester from that area who was with me, mentioned that there were some big rainbows in that stretch. He said I should take a fly rod, even though I was planning to fish the bass with plugs. That sounded good, and I did, but it proves how hidebound we are by tradition. Neither of us paused to wonder why the fly rod was necessary.

Partway along on the float, which was a rugged and sometimes frightening one, we saw a fish feeding. We argued as to whether it was a smallmouth or one of those rainbows. I was inclined to think the latter. Strengberg held out for bass. We both agreed it was big. I cast a slow-sinking wobbler across the path of the feeding fish, and as the plug ran deep into his view he smashed it. I muffed hooking him, however, and he went down.

We were having trouble with the tremendously swift current, and fought the boat into an eddy just below to take a rest. Presently the fish began feeding again. Convinced now that it was a bruiser of a smallmouth, I flung plugs at it for half an hour. No dice; it wasn't going to get nipped twice. Still it continued to feed.

Strengberg urged me to try a bug. I strung the fly rod and lambasted the big devil with popping bugs. It paid no heed. Suddenly I decided that no bass would pass up those bugs. I tied on a big spent-wing caddis, let the fish feed up toward me, dropped the fly a foot before its nose — and twenty minutes later, after a rousing fight, we netted a tremendous rainbow! True, it wasn't caught on a plug, but it came mighty close. It wasn't the trout's fault.

During that same float we saw a big swirl in a deep, black bend of the stream. I had on a frog-type bass plug. I cast ahead of the boat at the swirl, and wound up a beautiful bird's nest on my reel. With quick presence of mind Strengberg forced the boat into the slack eddy, then tossed overboard the log chain we sometimes dragged on a rope to slow us down. Thus anchored, I picked out the backlash. Meanwhile the plug, a sinker, had descended into the black eddy in quiet water beneath a rock wall.

Without thinking of fish, I wound up the slack and motioned to Mike to pull up the chain. As the line came tight, moving the frog off bottom, something slammed it viciously. I slammed back and swore in astonishment. The fish didn't jump; so neither of us even thought of trout. In fact, by the long feel of it as it lashed and ran crazily in the swift, black water I had pike in mind, which are in the quieter sections of the river. But when I finally licked the wild devil and brought it to the boat, Mike reached down and netted a rainbow that would go possibly 5 pounds. It was as black as the water from which it came.

Since then I've taken quite a number of trout on plugs. On very small plugs, cast with a fly rod, some have been small trout, some large. On plugs castable with a plug rod, they have invariably been big ones. I don't say plugging for trout should replace other methods of fishing, but I do say that here is a field of angling not sufficiently explored, and I believe it should interest many anglers, especially the legions of so-so fly casters and the strictly plug-rod men.

There is much to note here about technique. I have had big trout hit plugs when they were bottom-feeding; the strike comes the moment a plug, sunk to bottom and allowed to lie a moment, is moved. I might add, too, that this incident took place in the fall.

A lot more might be known today about trout versus plugs were it not for the trends in modern angling history. For some years manufacturers heavily pushed pint-sized replicas of their killer bass plugs, calling them "fly-rod plugs" and recommending them for trout. But they never got far, except in a couple of specialized instances, because such plugs are too awkward to cast with a fly rod. Later on tackle

Good brown trout fast to a bass plug. Close-up shows plug in mouth.

makers were doing something about that. The extra-long, extra-whippy plug rod was coming into its own; but before it had a real chance, spinning took over, which dimmed the chances of the whippy plug rod and light plug combo. Today some long, light plug rods are popular, but not for trout.

Now obviously spinning tackle does just as well as the plug rod. But particularly nowadays with bass so popular, there are a lot of hold-outs on spinning. So-called bait-casting tackle is basic to most large-lake bass fishing. In addition, there are scads of non-fly fishermen and always will be. To

And here's the proof that it can be done.

these and the non-spinners, I suggest that they shouldn't feel like hiding behind the alders when caught on trout waters with a bass outfit. And they shouldn't pass up trout waters because they're casting-reel addicts. A light-action 5½- or 6-foot plug rod, a fast reel, a light or medium line, and a collection of small and medium plugs will do a marvelous business for them, especially in the big rainbow and brown departments.

About five years ago I spent a month camping and fishing mostly for browns. It was midsummer, with quiet, warm, muggy nights. That is the time when you can simply murder immense browns — browns you'd never guess at other times were in the stream. I would pick a hole and fish it after dark with big flies in the orthodox fashion. I got hold of some awful trout, and landed several, but most of them I simply could not hold.

I reasoned that if fly monstrosities would arouse them after dark at that time, then they'd smash anything. I had often seen them jump for bats. So I got out the casting rod and some medium-sized surface bass plugs that would make a racket. I cast down and across, exactly as you'd fish a streamer. I raked the plugs slowly across the holes. And I raised and hooked some tremendous fish.

In my experience, choice of plugs should run to the smaller models, and for rainbows should shy from the more gaudy colors. Scale finishes, silvery plugs and small frog replicas are my pets. The two exceptions are yellow or orange, small with plenty of action, or black with spots. On the whole, the more natural-appearing the plug — minnowlike or froglike — the better. For browns, which are ordinarily the most wary of all trout, absolutely anything will do when the big boys are on the prod at dusk.

One year, three fly-fishermen friends of mine, using flies and bait, came in completely skunked. I followed one of them downstream with a fast-action plug rod. Casting a moderate-sized, deep-running, minnowlike jointed plug, I caught the only two fish of the day: both browns of around 2 pounds. For the beginner at this game, it's well to remember that the retrieve should be slow. Plugs should be fished no faster in swift current than streamer flies. Down-and-across casts are better than straight-downstream casts. Casts into eddies where sinking plugs will hit bottom and travel there slowly for a distance, finally swinging out into the current, are tops. The deep-diving and sinking plugs are far better than shallow-running ones, except in the case of browns after dark in hot weather.

If further proof of plug effectiveness on big trout is needed, the following incident should cinch it. Knowing that big rainbows are often most easily taken very early in the morning, I got up at four one fall day. We were stopping in a cabin on the bank of the Michagamme, an Upper Peninsula stream in Michigan that really runs downhill. Because of downstream rapids and rocks, I was afraid to put in the boat. I planned streamer flies from the bank for either big rainbows or smallmouths.

As I was setting up, a real old settler rolled nearby. I didn't want that fish to move off before I threw something at him. In the hazy dawn I grabbed for a plug rod all set up, with a small black-and-yellow bass plug dangling. Michagamme water is very dark. The plug somehow looked right to me. Hastily I heaved the little bass-killer beyond the swirl and retrieved it to bring it across what I hoped was the path of the feeding fish. There was no hesitation. As it swung into the current and laboriously wriggled upstream, running deep, the fish smashed it.

He came boiling up in a fantastic, tackle-rattling leap. I let out a whoop that woke the camp. The rod tip sizzled down to the grass tips, the fish raced around rocks, sounded, leaped, cartwheeled, all but came ashore in its frenzy to pick that triple-stinger out of its teeth. When it finally lay on the bank, with the plug hooks twisting my net into a horrible mess, I stared down at a rainbow that later tipped the scale at 6 pounds, gutted!

So try this sport, you pluggers. I don't guarantee you'll get as many trout as the spinners and the fly boys, but when you do hang one your chances of having it for your very own will be better than theirs. And for size, it'll match or better anything they'll bring in!

13

The Yellow Bass:
The Fish Nobody Knows

Some years ago I launched a rather pretentious fishing project. My goal: to fish for and catch every U.S. freshwater
species that could be considered game.

It wasn't long before I hit a snag. The yellow bass.

I knew very little about it. The more I sought information, the more I realized, to my amazement, that the little I
knew seemed to be about the extent of what was in print.

Today I know quite a lot more. I know the yellow bass
is probably the least-known of all our game fish, and that
some of the things written about it, even in the scientific
books, are wrong. I know that the modest-sized yellow bass
is one of the finest fighters of any fish that ever lived, and
that it is one of the most adaptable to the varied wiles of

anglers. It is a beautifully turned little piscatorial trickster, and a gourmet's delight.

None of this was easy to find out. When I first began to suspect difficulties, my curiosity was aroused. I hired a researcher to comb through 500-odd back issues of seven different magazines dealing with the outdoors. The information gleaned could have been noted on a postcard. One small item stated that the fish called "barfish" in the South, from its habit of schooling on shoals and bars, was the yellow bass. There was one pen drawing of a yellow bass, with caption. That was all. Later, one full-length story was unearthed. This dearth struck me as astonishing.

While this search was progressing, I combed through several dozen books about fishing and fish. The books about fishing mostly avoided quite studiously any mention of the yellow bass. A few gave it a paragraph or two, but dusted it off so lightly that I surmised their authors never had caught one.

The more scientific books about fish did better. They told me this species ranged from Indiana and southern Wisconsin and Minnesota through Iowa and south into Texas and Louisiana. True enough. They said it was abundant especially in the Mississippi Valley. They should have said "locally abundant." Yellow bass waters are never abundant. They are scattered.

They said it averages a pound to 2 pounds in weight. It doesn't. It averages less than a pound. There may be obscure waters where 1- and 2-pound yellow bass are the rule. In general, however, yellow bass run about the weight of good-sized bluegills. They are a longer and less compressed fish, and not as deep in the body. But they certainly fight as well as any bluegill, and that's a rare compliment.

The yellow bass belongs to the sea bass family. It and its close cousin, the white bass, are undoubtedly related to the saltwater striper. The white perch of fresh and brackish waters along the Atlantic Coast is also a close relative of the yellow bass. These three—white bass, yellow bass, white perch—are the U.S. freshwater representatives of the sea bass family.

Yellow bass are inhabitants of large rivers and medium-to-large lakes. They are, so the books say, predominantly Southern fish. Louisiana is supposed to be yellow bass head-quarters. And there are supposed to be records of 5-pounders. All of these book facts I doubt. I talked to about as many Louisiana natives who had never heard of them as native anglers elsewhere. I have located and caught more in the North than in the South, and have come to the conclusion that distribution is about equal. Nowhere did I ever find anyone who had seen an authentically recorded 5-pounder. Do they grow that big? I would like to know. A yellow bass that size would be sensational on light tackle.

In fact, in combing through the scientific books I soon suspected that each had researched the one before it. All said the same few things. None added anything new.

Yellow bass are very beautiful fish. They are silvery on the belly, distinctively brassy-yellow upward, sometimes almost canary yellow. Along the back this yellow becomes greenish to olive. Usually when the fish are pulled from the water, the fins, especially the lower fins, are a gorgeous shade of translucent powder blue.

There are seven (sometimes one more, or one less) dark or jet-black horizontal stripes running along each side. The stripes are not all continuous. They are broken, as if this little convict was untidy about his uniform.

These broken stripes are an identifying characteristic of the yellow bass, separating it from the white bass. But most of the reference books, I found, repeated over and over a glaring error about the stripes. They claimed only the lower ones are broken.

This is not so. Actually, and oddly, there is no rhyme or reason to the pattern formed by the stripes. One fish may have every stripe broken until it looks like a jumble. One may have only the upper ones broken. Often a stripe may have such a curious break that it forms a boxlike design midway. This lack of uniformity is an unusual thing in nature. Further, and more curious, it is not at all unusual to find individual yellow bass on which each side differs radically in pattern from the other. In fact, few have both sides identical.

Some books have stated that the yellow bass grows larger than the white bass. If this ever was true, it is now long outdated. White bass are a fine fish, and have been handled extensively by conservation departments, especially in impounded waters. I have caught them where they

Catch of yellow bass shows the varying markings on their sides.

averaged 2 pounds and went to 4. In these same waters, or waters nearby, yellow bass were very small. But they were, as some books have suggested, comparably better fighters.

Usually when white and yellow bass are in the same waters, since both feed avidly on minnows as well as aquatic insects, they compete directly for food. One species is bound soon to dominate. Quite often the yellow bass wins. Unfortunately, since it breeds very fast, it needs hard fishing, and if it doesn't get it, the fish soon are too numerous, and stunted. Reelfoot Lake in Tennessee is a good example. The Tennessee River also has yellow bass, called "yellow jacks," or "jacks" locally, that are mostly too small to be taken seriously.

My search for information was no more puzzling than my search for the fish themselves. In Alabama an old man told me the "streakers" weren't biting, and he didn't rightly know where to find them anyway. Elsewhere I met with shrugs about "yellow perch" and "streaks."

I had just about decided this couldn't be much of a fish, since almost nothing had been written about it over the years, fishermen seldom spoke of it, and most of them, in fact, didn't even know what it was. Then I had a letter from Mr. Jack Stevens, an Iowa conservation officer.

Mr. Stevens told me that if I would come to the town of Clear Lake, Iowa, where he was stationed, my yellow bass difficulties would be ended. I went. I found Clear Lake a thriving resort center. I found literally swarms of people converging on it from far and near for the sole purpose of catching a string of the unique little gamesters that Clear Lake offered in true abundance. And I found this untidy little convict a lightweight delight.

It seemed that Clear Lake was a kind of yellow bass headquarters. Everybody in the region, which is in northern Iowa not far from Mason City, knew the fish well and loved to catch and eat it. Because yellow bass spawn in spring—usually about May in Iowa—and gather in large concentrations then, I had hit the place at a fine time. I discovered that the lake was large, over 3,600 acres. I didn't know the first thing about catching this fish, and Mr. Stevens wasn't there just then, so I had to start out alone.

I began by casting from shore near a trailer park where we had parked our traveling home. I was using light spinning tackle, and a small spoon. Instantly I began getting strikes, but for one reason or another I didn't hook a single fish. Of course, I didn't know if the strikes were from the quarry I sought. It seemed to me the strikes were short. Maybe it would be better to use some kind of bait. The bait most easily available in a hurry was worms. Even though I suspected these fish, like their relatives, would be predominantly minnow feeders, I got some worms, rented a small boat, and blindly went after them.

After all the scratching around I'd done, I was genuinely excited over the prospects, even though I didn't expect big fish. Big doesn't necessarily mean proportionally more fun. I rigged up a homely old device—a small bell sinker at line's end, a dropper tied in a foot above, which carried hook baited with worm. I drifted on a gentle breeze, the time about 8 a.m., made a cast and just let the sinker slowly drag bottom. I could picture the bait twirling and tumbling along. But only for a few short seconds. There was a jerk on the line, the rod tip heeled down. A fish had hooked itself.

It took off like a turpentined cat, doggedly fighting near bottom, keeping the wispy rod dramatically curled. I liked that. I liked the feel of this fish. It just had to be my first yellow bass, at last. Presently I had it up where I could see it in the clear, cold water. Sure enough. Quickly I had it into the boat where I could stare at it with immense satisfaction, and get the feel of it in hand.

A farmer fishing with a cane pole taught me a trick that worked wonders.

I was to learn that worms are by no means the best bait. Minnows are far better. One can also even cut up sizable baitfish, using cut bait. But it was an old hand, a farmer who lived nearby and whom I saw standing quietly among reeds and fishing with a cane pole, who taught me quite a bait trick. He was having excellent luck. He explained that he used any bait he could get to catch the first one. Then he cut the throat latch out of it. This is the triangular section of the throat below the mouth. It is very tough. Once on a hook, it won't easily come off. It appears white in the water, waves teas-

158

Above: I discovered a line of fly fishermen having success, and I eagerly joined in.

Right: Kids with crude tackle are delighted with yellow bass, too.

ingly when reeled on a dropper rig such as I was using, and for some reason the yellow bass just can't resist it. I caught ten fish on a single bait before it became too chewed up.

That was not all I learned. That evening I saw a line of anglers wading and fly-fishing off the rocky shore of a small island. They were having a great time of it. Since fly-fishing has always been a favorite method of mine, I got into the act in a hurry. I learned that during spawning these fish, which do not fan a nest but simply deposit and fertilize eggs over gravel bars or along rocky shores, swarm in the shallows. They are, incidentally, also school fish year round, so when you find one you've invariably found a stringerful. But not only do they concentrate inshore during spawning. They do the same when heavy mayfly hatches are on, and at such times feed on both nymphs and mature flies.

I waded, trying first streamers, then wet flies, and even just to see what might happen, small bluegill popping bugs. If I thought the light spin tackle added stature to this fish, I soon knew that a fly rod added more. They struck swiftly and hard, fought with keen determination. I was told that all summer long the evening fishing in shallows is usually good.

Of course, during summer and on into the fall, trolling is a good way to locate schools. Then one can stop and cast to them. I experimented with small minnowlike plugs, with spinner and feather, and more with small spoons. The yellow bass didn't discriminate. They hit them all.

Curiously, the fish was not known in Clear Lake, or at least was very rare, during the first decades of this century. But then white bass were common. Suddenly, in the 1930s, yellow bass started to show up in numbers. The white bass almost disappeared. This same phenomenon of ups and downs has occurred several times.

I was so interested in having found and experienced this doughty little fish that after we had settled down in Texas some years back I stopped for a retake at Clear Lake during a summer trip. Alas, the prime fishing was no more. There were yellow bass all right—by millions. They had over-populated, and become stunted. At that time muskellunge had even been stocked in the lake to see if they could whittle the yellow bass down.

Certainly this fish is not rare. But it is nonetheless difficult to locate. In recent years I discovered it again in Caddo Lake up in the extreme northeast corner of Texas, a lake shared with Louisiana and an interesting jungle of moss-hung cypress and aquatic plants. It is in several Texas streams—the Red which forms the border with Oklahoma, the Cypress and the Sabine. Lake Tawakoni, which is on the upper Sabine River drainage, has swarms of them, along with some buster black bass, and locals even fish heavily for them in spring and summer.

The closely related white bass has become an incredibly abundant and popular species as building of large impound-ments—a perfect habitat—has progressed in past years. White bass have been stocked far and wide with startling success. But oddly enough, attempts to stock and establish yellow bass in waters where they're not native both within the rather restricted range and outside it have had virtually no success. In addition, experiments in propagation, suc-cessful with white bass, also have failed.

So if you're going to try for this fish nobody seems to know, you'll have to hunt for it, just as I did. I've located a couple of waters in Louisiana that actually do have them, just like the old books said. And there, again by the book, I found local fishermen calling them "barfish." Even though the species is small—maybe it's a "panfish" and not a "game fish," which makes little difference anyway—the experience of catching it is sporty indeed, and it is a superb little critter in a skillet.

14

Primer for the New Pike Fisherman

Southern Manitoba can be crisp even in mid-June. On a blowy spring morning we were 40 water miles back in huge Whiteshell Provincial Park, bundled in wool shirts and nylon windbreakers. In two boats we cruised up the Winnipeg River looking for a good bay for pike. We were producing a TV film. When you're engaged in this endeavor excuses don't count. You catch fish or else!

"Let's check here," Chuck Danforth shouted from the other boat.

A bay opened and distantly down its shoreline reeds were visible. Chuck, retired, had been one of the country's top tackle reps. With him was tackle manufacturer Dick Kotis. My son, Terry, and I were in the second boat with photographer Ebb Warren.

Chuck snapped on a large, heavy spoon, let it down to

bottom, raked it quickly along, then reeled up. "Just right," he called. "About 10 feet at most and weeds on bottom." He pulled trailing vegetation from the lure.

They began casting toward the rocky shore, letting the spoons settle close to the unseen vegetation. Soon Chuck reared back, hitting a fish with a jolting strike. The rod, arced high above him, surged downward. Line peeled away. The breeze sang across it as it lengthened at surface, and suddenly the fish exploded, wallowing, throwing water wildly. It looked like 10 pounds. Ebb's camera was whirring. Excitement crackled among us.

As Chuck finally brought his fish under control, Dick laced into one off the bow. A twin to Chuck's, it came flying out in a burst of action, leaping high, falling with a flat-sided *splatt* that fairly echoed off the rocks.

Camera still going, Ebb muttered happily, "Talk about luck!"

But we both knew this had nothing to do with luck. Within two hours we managed to put a dozen fish on film. It was possible because our "actors" knew precisely where and how to find and catch our quarry.

Many fishermen nowadays need to know those details — the new crop of anglers who vacation in Canada, where sport fishing has so swiftly developed and pike are a mainstay, the fishermen who visit or live in the numerous states that have pike available today where once they were few or not present at all. Years ago it was faddish to call pike "snakes" or "trash." No longer. They're big and they're vicious fighters. Trying for trophy pike has become an important facet of modern fishing.

Much of this is due to the vast spread in range and new waters. Originally pike were found across most of Canada, and from a few east-Montana streams and small lakes of the Dakotas to the St. Lawrence. The center of U.S. pike fishing was in the Great Lakes region and eastward. Now it has moved west. Dams on the Missouri River have formed huge lakes — Fort Peck in Montana, Sakakawea, Oahe, Sharpe, Francis Case, Lewis & Clark down across the Dakotas to northeast Nebraska — that stretch almost a thousand miles and are considered presently perhaps the most important single pike fishery on the continent. More fishermen are learning about this. Scads of 10- to 20-pounders and a few 30 to 35 are caught annually.

Further, biologists have been successfully stocking pike as predator fish to help control undesirable species in numerous waters and states where none previously existed. Far western Montana has some. Wyoming has launched a program. Nebraska is utilizing new waters for them. Kansas now offers pike fishing. But most startling, so do Colorado, Arizona, New Mexico, Oklahoma and Texas! The pike is no longer a "Northern."

Recently in Colorado a fisherman said to me, "Did you hear about that 31-pound pike caught in our state? I'd sure like to try them but haven't the faintest idea how."

I'd heard the same sentiment voiced by first-timers from the States visiting in Canada, anglers who'd never been exposed to pike. And I'd heard it in Montana, the Dakotas, and New Mexico both from visitors and natives. It's understandable that one's first attempts at catching a species new to him should be puzzling. Where I live, in Texas, for example, everyone has long fished chiefly for bass and catfish. The few who've tried pike get mighty perplexed.

Pike aren't hard to catch. In fact, they're savage and under proper conditions eager strikers. But you do have to understand their habits, preferences and whimsies. A common allusion to pike is that "they'll eat anything that moves." Forget that. Experimentation with baits and lures isn't necessary. The diet of adult pike is almost entirely made up — 90-plus percent — of other fishes, taken *alive*. Whatever fish are predominantly present will be the mainstay of diet. This automatically dictates what bait or lures to use, and that lure movement is mandatory.

For example, in Canada one summer I fished a lake that had only pike and walleyes. Walleyes, up to a foot long, were what the pike lived on. I used a big spoon, copper inside and perch finish outside, to mimic the flash and basic colors of a walleye. It was murder. In a New Mexico lake, pike were stocked to clean out suckers interfering with rainbow trout production. The pike mopped up the suckers, started on the rainbows. Silvery and red-and-white spoons were taken most readily there when I fished it. Where a variety of forage is present, almost any active lure attracts pike. They're not very selective. But when forage variety is lacking, results are at least mildly enhanced by trying to imitate what is present.

I had the excitement and valuable experience of fishing much for pike as a youngster, in the Flint River, once a lovely farm-country bottomland stream but now ruined, in the "Thumb" area of Michigan. My first trials, of course, were with cane pole. I learned much about pike from an old gentleman, Josh McGuigan, who often fished along the river near where we lived.

"Big bait, big pike," he told me.

Tiny pike may slam large lures. But mature pike, where food is plentiful, grab a stomachful per lunge rather than working hard for tidbits. Four-inch spoons beat 2-inch spoons. One day Mr. McGuigan caught an 8-inch sucker on a worm.

He said, "Let me fix you a riggin', son. See if you can catch a big fish."

From his tobacco-tin tackle box he dug out a stout hook, and a bolt for a sinker. He whittled a large bobber from a stick. Then he hooked the sucker through the lips and helped

Pike like big lures, just as
they like big forage. In un-
hooking these fish, watch
those teeth as well as the
hooks.

me place it in a quiet back eddy of the slow river, in tree shade with arrowhead clumps bordering the pool. The water was perhaps 3 feet deep.

"A big pike stays there," he said. "I've lost him twice."

As the sucker pulled the big bobber around, it suddenly took a wild dive and didn't come up.

"Let him get it good!" Mr. McGuigan commanded. Then at last, "Now! Yank hard!"

I laid back and thought the whole river had blown up. I'd like to say I proudly dragged the brute home. The fact was, after several violent charges and splashes it cut my salt-and-pepper line as neatly as with shears. This was a lesson. Wire leaders of 6 or 8 inches — which weren't around then — are recommended. I've landed a good many on heavy, hard nylon, which slips fairly well over the mass of backward-slanted teeth without cutting, but it's far from invulnerable.

From that very first experience I learned also that pike are lurkers. They move some, of course, traveling especially during early spring spawning right after ice-out. But they're fashioned chiefly for short bursts of incredible speed, with jaws equipped for inextricably trapping forage. A pike is built like a projectile. Large specimens require much food, will select a lair and stay in the vicinity as long as food, cover and water temperature are constant.

In Manitoba Chuck Danforth told me, "Many fishermen consider pike difficult. But they simply don't get their lures to them pinpoint. A pike may follow a lure, once it spots it, right to the boat before striking. But you have to make lots of casts to be sure the lure goes to where each fish lies in wait. You can troll parallel to cover rather effectively. But that's dull sport. Parallel casting is smart, however."

Because they're lurkers that ambush prey, pike are *always* in close contact with cover. That's the most impor-

167

tant fact to learn about them. On occasion logs, rocks, shoals or bars may serve, but *vegetation*—reeds, lily pads, even short bottom growth, whatever is available—is where most pike are most of the time. The dorsal and anal fins, set far back at tail base and without spines, and the snout and body shape are all designed beautifully for swift acceleration and shooting through vegetative cover like a rocket.

When Chuck Danforth dropped the big spoon to bottom in that Manitoba bay, he was weed hunting. "If none had been present," he told me later, "we'd have moved up the bay to the reeds. But the mouth, I knew, past which some river current could be felt, was the spot where most sizable forage would be found. Pike would lie just out of the current, waiting—as long as weed cover was present."

Pike are not deep-water fish. On occasion in certain lakes in warm weather, or because of some particular forage, they may take refuge at 30 or even 50 feet. But that's a very specialized situation. Depths from 2 or 3 to 12 or 15 feet catch 90 percent of them.

An Arizona friend recently told me he was having difficulty with this introduced fish in his state. "Do they act differently down here?" he asked.

I assured him they did not. Pike are pike, anywhere.

He said, "I've tried night fishing, figuring they'd be cruising in the open then."

That, I explained, was an error. Pike do not feed after dark, and little in low light. Latitude and time of year, of course, control hours of daylight and darkness. On the average, heavy feeding begins about eight a.m., assuming it's daylight then. Food taken the previous afternoon has digested during the night. With empty stomachs, pike are generally most eager during the morning, until well on toward noon. Action then ceases or slows till mid-p.m., when the fish must begin stoking up again for the night fasting period.

A most confusing facet of pike fishing for modern anglers concerns water temperature. It shuts action on and off perhaps more emphatically than for any other freshwater game fish. I remember as a kid fishing one chilly April day with my first casting tackle, a truly garbled-up outfit with which I awkwardly cast a plug I'd whittled, painted and equipped with hooks. I caught four pike in the Flint River. I didn't get a chance to fish again until July. Anticipation was frenzied. My homemade plug, I knew, would slay 'em again. But I didn't catch the first one. Only rock bass would hit.

Years later, during my first fishing trip into Canada, in midsummer, we caught cords of pike. But when I returned home to southern Michigan and tried pike haunts I knew, not a one would hit. Eventually I learned that pike prefer, and are most active in, water of 50 to 60 degrees. Above 65, feeding slows considerably, and pike won't stay in their shallow-water haunts. They become scattered, "homeless," difficult to locate, and anglers also have to compete with the superabundant summer crop of young forage fish.

In Canada, where shallows may remain cool all summer, pike stay in their regular haunts, concentrated and catchable. Farther south, summer pike fishing gets more and more difficult. This is one reason fishing in the new Western and Southwestern waters perplexes anglers. The coldest months, when fewer fishermen are out, offer the best opportunity. In warm months high temperatures dampen action. Pike can tolerate and thrive in warmer waters of the Southwest, but are fundamentally a cold-water species.

Altitude adds to the confusion. In west-central Montana one hot summer I fished a series of shallow pike lakes near Choteau almost to no avail. But in a small, deep lake farther

While Manitoba angler tries to get net, pike dances at boatside.

west and much higher, with water temperature consequently lower, I licked several good fish. In New Mexico several years ago I had a whizzer of a pike session in August, stringing fish to 8 and 10 pounds. But the lake lay at 7,000 feet and night air temperature dropped into the high 30s.

At Colorado's Vallecito Reservoir, as this is written the state's best pike water, I was able to catch pike along with trout and kokanee. This, too, was in August. But again, altitude was 7,500 feet and weather crisp. Conversely, in Texas, Oklahoma, Kansas, and Nebraska the summer weeks, no question, can be most discouraging for pike fishermen. A useful key in this respect to pike personality is that the species is active all winter, a mainstay of ice fishing. Small pike can even be stocked through holes in the ice in winter with no ill effects. I checked all last year the reports from some of the top pike lakes along the Missouri in the Dakotas. The cold months when ice fishermen were out, and

Above: For really wild action, try pike on streamer flies. This scene is in Montana. *Below:* A good one about played out and ready to take in.

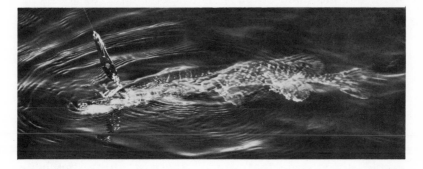

the early spring and the fall months furnished a preponderance of the catch, and of the trophy fish.

Where water temperatures around the year never fall extremely low, pike growth is astonishing. This is one reason there are high hopes for outsize pike eventually in the Southwest. One of the Oklahoma biologists working with them told me recently they had authenticated growth in a single year, in a lake where temperature allows year-round growth, from fingerling to over 3 pounds! It's not quite that fast in the North, but pike do grow faster than other freshwater game fish. That's a clue for anglers, too. Swift growth requires an uncommon rapacity, and gluttony. Food intake of a 5-pounder is at least 1 pound daily, of a 10-pounder double that, and so on. Thus if you know pike cover and get the lure to the fish, under proper temperature conditions, you can hardly fail.

What lures? If you're a bait fisherman, use minnows 4 to 6 inches long. If you're a plug fisherman, use husky diving or sinking plugs for average fishing, chugger surface types for great sport when pike are in very shallow water. If you're a metal-lure addict, spinner and bucktail (or feather) will do well, but the plain old-fashioned spoon three to six inches long, in varied colors suitable to varied waters and forage present, will catch pike for you consistently the rest of your days. I've made numerous successful trips on which I carried nothing but spoons, a selection of several weights, sizes, colors, including a few weedless models and a few with feather attached.

If pike are abundant I like to use single hooks rather than trebles. Fish are easier to release. For "keepers" the treble saves some that would otherwise throw the hook. Color choice depends on two items: clarity or stain of the water, and what forage fish are present. In cloudy or heavily stained Northern waters, bright flashers are needed so they show up well. In clear unstained waters, less flash is necessary. Where forage species may be varied, any color may do well. Change until you hit a lure that seems productive. Red-and-white is a great standard, although I've no idea why it should be so productive. Possibly it's just because of high visibility. If forage is limited to one or two species, match these with reasonable accuracy and your results will always be better.

If you happen to be adept with fly-fishing equipment, or are a spin fisherman used to using a water-filled bubble, by all means try streamer flies for pike. This is unquestionably the ultimate in sport with this species. At Fort Peck Reservoir in Montana a few seasons back I had a furiously active day with pike on big yellow-and-red and perch-imitator streamers, using a fly rod and heavy monofil leader. Fish of 3 pounds, hooked in 3 feet of water over weed beds in quiet, small bays, leaped far more formidably than trout. When a brute of 10 pounds or more sucked in my streamer, in plain sight of the boat, I felt like giving up right there.

The fish steamed away like a submarine, hit the end of the tether, paused. Then, suddenly realizing it was tied up, it took to the air. I had it on for two jumps in those snug quarters and haven't seen it since. In open waters in Canada I've done better with big ones, using heavier fly-fishing equipment.

That, of course, is specialized fishing. The spoon or plug fished with sturdy bait-casting tackle, such as a "worming" rod and a star-drag reel, or light saltwater spin tackle, is standard pike equipment. And remember, although you may catch a swarm of baby pike in a short stretch of a reed bed, adult pike are solitary except during spring spawning. Don't expect more than one trophy from a specific location, although in big water, such as that mentioned earlier in Manitoba, another may have its lair 30 to 50 yards distant.

Our best morning on that trip occurred when Ebb Warren, the cameraman, and I quit work and fished too. We'd discovered a channel perhaps 40 yards wide and a quarter-mile long leading from one lake to another. Reeds grew at either end, and lined some of the banks. This set-up—and remember it well—is one of the most perfect that ever occurs. Such channels are natural travel and hiding places for forage fish. They are quiet and secluded, and pike often in swarms reside in them. As we drifted and tossed spoons, pike after pike slammed them. Most were fish of 3 or 4 pounds, a few were much larger.

After a while Terry and Ebb and I went ashore to get some photos of the other boat from a high point. We took a rod and net. Sparse submerged vegetation grew on rocks near where we disembarked. We walked down a bit and I began casting. Across the channel we could see that Chuck had a good fish on. Then suddenly a pike stopped my big spoon cold. Line streaked off my heavy spinning reel. I did not have a steel leader on and was certain I'd lose the fish. Because this was an interlude of sport on a working trip, I desperately wanted at least one trophy.

After possibly ten minutes, I was leading it gingerly to shore. At the last instant it gave a massive heave. I slacked off. Miraculously, it was still hooked. Finally Terry slipped the net under it and I had my trophy fish of the trip — not any record, but slightly over 15 pounds. For closing action of a great water journey in wonderful wilderness country it was good enough for me. There are many like it waiting for fishermen all the way from Canada almost to the Mexican border nowadays. I hope the "primer" I've put together here out of long experience will help you hang one on your wall!

15

Sharp as a Cutlass

The cutlass fish is a weird-looking creature with an expression, mouth open, like some demon from prehistoric times. It has teeth like spikes, and a snake-like, supple body form that allows it to swim with an undulating motion. It is so long and thin that it looks very much like a snake in the water, especially because it has a pencil-skinny tail. But the name, of course, originated because someone long ago thought this silvery blade of a fish resembled the shape and appearance of a cutlass.

Few, if any, anglers purposely fish for the cutlass. Although it is claimed as edible, our family tried it and decided that whoever said so must either have been a little loose with the truth or mighty hungry. To be sure, it won't kill you, but I doubt anybody would go back for seconds. Yet what this odd fish lacks on the table, it more than makes up for in crystal-pure sport at the end of a line, for those who'll seek it. It is one of the wildest leapers and violent battlers imaginable.

Vividly I recall the first one I ever hooked. I was fishing a channel with a metal spoon, running it along bottom slowly, hoping for a flounder. I was using light spinning tackle. The spoon stopped with a jolt. I struck back, the rod heeled over, and I could sense a severe struggle of something that must be long and lean, down there 10 or 15 feet. Then line started coming up, and a silver-and-platinum lance shot from the water surface, flailing and gyrating in midair, seeming to furl and unfurl.

It fell to the water and went up again. And again. Then it splashed and protested as I cranked away. Because of its exceedingly compressed and flexible build, the cutlass cannot sustain a battle for a long period. It does not have the solid muscle. But it is a most primitive, violent sort for a couple of minutes. And it is under certain circumstances, when ganged up, a most willing striker.

This is a species that hangs out in marine cuts and seashore river mouths of the lower Atlantic and the Gulf coasts. There is also a Pacific variety in the family, and also one called a scabbardfish, of the Pacific. Its close-in habits put the cutlass within casting distance rather often of shore-bound anglers. As I've said, seldom does anyone try purposely to catch it. And usually when an angler unwittingly hooks one he is astonished and not just sure what he's hung. Fact is, all too commonly the cutlass is called a ribbonfish. This is incorrect. The ribbonfishes belong to another family entirely.

Nonetheless, that name dies hard. Along the Texas coast it is thoroughly established. Here the species is much used by bait dealers. It is sliced up and frozen and is a popular cut bait for numerous purposes. The bait gatherers often concentrate on it during winter, especially when the weather is chilly. At such times large schools of "ribbonfish" gather in deep holes that are protected, where water temperature is warmer than elsewhere. They cannot tolerate low temperatures, have been dubbed "frostfish" in some locations, where during cold snaps they often can be picked up, benumbed.

Weird-looking and good only for cut bait, the cutlass fish is nonetheless an outstanding experience on light tackle.

Like a flying silver lance, cutlass fish takes to the air. With leap after leap this curious customer gave a dramatic performance. The fish is so flexible it flails away in snakelike gyrations. When the fish is finally landed, I hold it to disengage the hook. They'll snap at you otherwise.

Left: My son Mike leans back to battle a big one. His largest fish measured 42 inches. *Right:* The cutlass has an astonishing mouthful of fangs.

One of my most interesting experiences with the cutlass fish occurred during just such a cold snap, at Port Aransas, Texas. I had taken my wife and my two boys there for a few days between Christmas and New Year's. The boys were then small, but nonetheless eager fishermen. I had promised them a couple of boat trips, one out into the Gulf, another in the bays. But the weather was so bad we couldn't get out at all. And the only place we could find that was at least a bit protected from a bitter wind was the sandy edge of a cut that ran up to the public boat ramp.

179

I had no idea what we might catch, but was willing to give anything a try, just to placate my disappointed offspring. On one of the first casts, with a spoon, Mike hooked a fish that gave him a startling tussle, with many high leaps. It was, of course, a cutlass, and when finally he had it beached he was so excited he started to run to grab it. I cautioned him. Commonly a cutlass on the beach or held in shallow water will eye you and leap to snap at your reaching hand. It pays to be very cautious. The teeth are truly fierce implements. I've watched them grind a metal lure as I tried with pliers to remove it.

Cutlass fish will take both lures and cut bait. They do not seem to be discriminating feeders. They grow occasionally to as much as 5 feet long. The largest we caught that day, which was a wild melee of fish constantly in the air, was one Mike landed that taped 42 inches. An interesting capability of the cutlass fish is that it can swim straight backward under full steam. Few fish can. You can see a demonstration of this by holding one on a lure just lightly enough so it can take line. The snakelike undulations reverse and the fish moves straight backward!

Ugly as they are, I have a pleasant attitude about cutlass fish. They've filled a gap for us on several occasions and given us great sport. They can do the same for any fisherman in their territory, especially at inclement times such as I've described. The photos we took that bitter day at Port Aransas will give you an idea of what unusual action this is.

16
How to Seduce a Fish

The man had on a pair of hip boots and a fishing vest. He came into the roadside store and gas station near Red River, New Mexico, and seemed in a hurry. It was nine a.m. I was waiting around, trying to get a tire repaired. The man rummaged in the small refrigerated case at the back of the store where milk, cheese and lunch meat were kept.

Presently he came to the cash register, slapped something down on the counter. "How much is this roll of garlic cheese?"

I shuddered. Garlic cheese at nine a.m.! The man hurried out and drove off. Five minutes later two others drove up, rushed into the store. "Got any garlic cheese?" one asked.

When they'd gone, I said to the lady taking care of the store, "Sure are a lot of garlic lovers around here."

Garlic cheese and pink-and-white marshmallows — what crazy ways to catch trout.

She smiled. "Oh, they don't eat it. They feed it to the trout. Didn't you know? It's the hottest bait ever. We sell bushels of it."

Now this sort of thing, admittedly, has sent many a purist angler into his padded cell to rave, pound the walls, and tear his hair. But as I discovered, the fact was that the garlic-cheese guys were just flat sacking up trout while the purists were doing almost nothing. I'm not convinced I want to get caught fishing with garlic cheese for trout. But it is true that scheming, ingenious anglers are constantly spawning crazy ideas that turn out to be the greatest fish catchers of all time.

Take the overalled, snuff-chewing gent I had one time as a guide on a back-swamp Florida lake. He sculled the boat oh so quietly up to the edge of a vast floating bed of water hyacinths. Then he picked up a long cane pole with no line on it, and after having been so quiet maneuvering into position, he began beating the tops of the hyacinths with his pole, making a terrible commotion.

I was startled. I thought perhaps he'd swallowed his snuff. "You'll scare every fish . . ." I began.

"Shhhhh!" he glowered at me. Then presently he ceased

his racket and sat back with an evil sort of smile. "We'uns'll jest wait a bit naow," he said.

We waited a bit. Then with extreme caution he reached out his paddle and swept a small hole in the floating vegetation. "Drop yore minner in thur," he commanded. "Easy."

I baited with a live minnow and eased it down through the opening in the hyacinths. It had wafted down only a short distance when something seized it and raced away. When line stopped running, I set the hook. I was into a tremendous bass.

When the fish was finally aboard and the excitement over, the old gent said, "See how I done it? I knock the whey outa the hyacinths. Bugs and worms in the roots and leaves fall and sink down to bottom. Lotsa small brim comes a-grabbin' 'em. Then old Mr. Bass he comes a-huntin' him a brim — and you gives him a minner with a hook in it!" He slapped his leg and cackled and allowed it was a right smart way to fish. I allowed it was a right smart way to fish, too.

There is something fresh and inspiring, in this packaged, well-labeled age, about the crazy and unorthodox antics of anglers determined to bring their finned quarry to bay. Millions of fishermen, to be sure, have succumbed to a computerized world. The tackle companies offer them full outfits, even with the knots properly tied to affix a lure, and they meekly accept. There are casting instructions on the box, and with the lure there is a set of directions as to how to fish it. Even the operation of the reel is so carefully programmed that you don't have to flip your noggin, you just flip a switch. You can even do this, literally, with an electric reel now on the market!

That in itself is a kind of reverse-kook. But it is the delightful applications of pure imagination — sometimes good horse sense, sometimes undoubtedly mumbo-jumbo — by the hardcore individualists among anglers that sets them apart in the genius category. Wacky or not, it is difficult to short-sell their results.

For example, a good many years ago I did my first saltwater fishing. This was in Florida. I knew utterly nothing about saltwater fishing. But I thought I was quite a hotshot freshwater man. Used to wading trout streams, I started out wading in Sarasota Bay, casting a lure. I didn't really know what I was fishing for, but I had hope.

Presently another fisherman waded in nearby. He had a heavy, stiff rod. On his line was a long bobber, its top dished out. Immediately below it he had placed a small sinker on the line. Then several feet lower, at the end, was a hook with a shrimp impaled. This curious contraption with sinker up below the cork I'd never seen before. Now he hurled the rig out and it hit with a big splatt. He let the bobber straighten up, then he began jerking his rod in short, sharp jerks. The dished top of the cork bobber made a loud slurping, popping noise. It was obvious to me that this dope knew nothing about fishing.

I sidled over, said, "I hope you won't mind if I point out that you'll scare off everything for a half-mile around in this shallow water doing that."

He turned and stared at me as if I had been washed ashore dead several days ago. About that time his bobber swooped under. He laid back on the rod and after a battle brought in a beautiful big sea trout. Amazed as well as embarrassed, I watched while he did it several more times.

Finally I said, "Okay. So I'm a big damn fool."

He grinned now, and went on to explain what he was doing. Sea trout, or weakfish, feed a great deal on live shrimp. Live shrimp hide in aquatic grass and vegetation on the flats. Flushed out by cruising fish, they start to swim and the trout belt one after another. In the shallows these vicious strikes make a surface noise — slurp, pop, slurp.

"By imitating the sound of feeding trout," the man explained — and he too had that satisfied, evil little glint all ingenious anglers seem to wear when an idea jells — "I attract feeding trout. They think other trout are grabbing shrimp. As one races to the sound, it sees my shrimp dancing along as I jerk the rod — and *whammo!* Pretty good, huh?"

It is interesting to note that undoubtedly the first fisherman who doped this idea out, years ago, was considered a kook by his cronies. Then they saw that it worked, and boy did they grab it. Today the "popping rod" and "popping cork" for this specialized fishing has for years been standard in any tackle store, and the method is murderous. Thus the oddball innovations of today often become the killers of tomorrow. Many, wacky as they may be, are still rather brilliant flashes of insight.

Every fisherman, I'm sure, has heard of the fox-sharp old woodsie who devised the "Great Mouse Trick." This crafty old cuss knew that an enormous pike had its lair near a submerged log out in the lake where he fished. But he could never get near enough to cast to the fish without alerting it. So, he caught a live mouse, tied his hook and line to the leg of the mouse. With the breeze just right, he now placed the mouse on a shingle and floated it out toward the log, meanwhile paying out slack line. When it was in position, with a snap of his rod he jerked the mouse off the shingle. The mouse swam desperately. Alas, Old Slabsides rose instantly from his hiding place and engulfed this mousy proposition with the string attached.

Some may say this never happened. I like to believe it did. And I can tell you one just as wacky that did happen because I was there, as a barefoot kid, and witnessed it. There was this old riverbank-sitting canepoler of our rural Michigan community who spent more time fishing than farming. I used to sneak off down to the slow-winding oxbow loops of the Flint River and watch him. He really knew how to haul 'em in.

"Son," he said one day when things were slow, "I'll show you how to ketch a green bass when they ain't bitin'."

First he hunted around and found a hollow grass stem. Then he caught a frog. I watched with some squeamishness now as he inserted the grass stem into the rectum of the frog, and blew it up. He knew, but I did not, that a poor frog thus inflated was unable readily to deflate itself. He now hooked the frog very lightly through a front leg, and with no sinker on his line tossed the frog out into a deep hole in a slow-currented bend. Unable to submerge, the frog tried to swim ashore. Before it got far there was a murderous swirl into which the frog disappeared. A smallmouth bass, which the old gent called "green bass," had it, and in a trice was heaved out upon the bank. Cruel, perhaps, but imaginative to say the least.

Sometimes in their frantic determination to catch fish, crafty anglers go to the kookiest lengths of all—cruelty to themselves. I laugh yet to think, for example, of my meeting with a young gent who, to save him embarrassment, I'll call John Smith. This was in Tennessee. He let me in on the secret of his success as a bass fisherman. He used big live worms, the kind called nightcrawlers. Some of them were almost of snake size.

That was not all he used. But not until after we left the dock in his boat did he give any hint of what was up. Too many people were watching. With the coast clear, he furtively but with some ceremony unlocked his tackle box and took a big, fresh package of leaf-type chewing tobacco from it. It made me wince to see the size of the wad he stuffed into his mouth. Wordlessly now, he ran the motor, heading for his favorite fishing hole. Conversation was impossible even with his chin up. His cud was immense. I was sitting up front, facing him. I thought he began first to look a little bit pale, and then green. He slowed, took out his cud, placed it on the seat beside him, leaned overboard and was horribly sick.

Finally we were at the spot. John continued to be sick intermittently. He looked awful. He was obviously suffering. But he got us baited up between sick spells and now, cud in place, he squirted a copious portion of tobacco juice onto each nightcrawler. Did they ever wriggle and squirm! I'd heard of spitting on a hook for luck, but not of marinating bait in tobacco juice to make it dance the kooch. Over the side they went.

John looked greenly at me but managed a triumphant leer. "You just watch," he said. "That'll fix 'em!"

I had a strike. So did John. We wrestled the two big bass and got them into the boat. John had his chaw laid on the seat now, using it only as needed to work up more marinade for the baits. Finally when that cud wore down, he hesitatingly got out a fresh wad, studied it fearfully, then steeled himself and started in on it. Soon he was sick all over again. This went on until we had limits.

On the way in I said, "John, I just don't understand how you can enjoy this."

"Well," he said, "I'll admit it makes me awful sick." Then came that happy leer again. "But don't it just catch the living hell out of the bass, though!"

Bright bursts of ingenuity seem to occur regularly with baits and lures. I knew a man in Wisconsin, a muskie addict, who would lie awake nights scheming how to catch a big one. He had observed that wild ducks trying to raise broods on one of the lakes he fished were constantly harassed by an enormous muskellunge he'd been after a long time. It gobbled the ducklings as fast as they hit the water.

"It made me mad," he told me. "I wanted the ducklings to grow up so I could shoot them come fall. I also desperately wanted that fish. The madder I got, the more I wanted revenge—and right there is where I hit this big idea."

What he did was to build a baby duck. It took a month of whittling, and of mechanical trial and error. But when he was through he had a replica that wouldn't quit. It even had feathers, feet that paddled as he reeled, and a head and neck that moved back and forth. It also had hooks on each foot.

He "swam" this crafty contraption back and forth, back and forth over the lie of the monster. "It looked so good," he said, "that a real duck even came to investigate—and the damn fish ate *it!*"

But he stayed with the scheme. And at last the muskie engulfed the man-made duckling in one smashing attack. The battle was fierce and prolonged. When it was finished, so was the muskie. Elation coursed through the angler. He had the answer forevermore. But now he looked at his lure. It was featherless, bodyless. It had been rent and utterly destroyed.

As he related all this, I said, "Couldn't you patent it and get mass production and really have something?"

That triumphant gleam leaped across his face. "Patent it hell!" he exploded. "All I wanted to do was fix that big bastard's wagon—and right there he is, on the wall!"

Such attitudes must be accepted, not reasoned. So must the patience that settles upon a fisherman who has been smitten with a stupendous idea. Well I recall when salmon eggs were outlawed as bait for steelhead trout during their runs on the streams of northern Michigan. All trout are to some extent spawn eaters. And too many big rainbows were being caught via the salmon-egg route.

The boom had lowered when one man, a kind of last straw, was observed standing on a bridge across the Sturgeon River for a whole day, intermittently tossing out by hand single salmon eggs into the current below. Several big trout down there in a pool just couldn't be caught. But this

Above left: Muskies have been the impetus for concoction of many a crackpot lure—like one run up by a friend who whittled a baby duck and outfitted it with feathers and feet that paddled when he reeled. *Top right:* Look what's been done to the old angleworm. Now they're not only plastic, but in rainbow hues. *Above right:* I corrected the man who was, I thought, scaring the sea trout with his noisy popping cork. Fact is, it's pure murder.

scheming gentleman had devised a plan. When he figured a trout was about full but still eager, he pitched over an egg with a small but strong hook buried in it, letting the nylon monofilament line waft down slack along with it. He could actually observe the big brute gulp the egg—and he caught every big one in the hole just that way.

When the salmon-egg ban hit, there was anguished moaning. But not for long. A kernel of corn soaked in Mercurochrome and then in fish oil was a dead ringer, smell and all. Worked, too. And when corn was in some places outlawed, well, heck, canned peas dyed pink or red were better replicas, although not as firm as the more discriminating kooks might have wished.

There is just no limit to the devious mental processes of the angle-minded angler. Some sort of mesmerism must attend fishing that blinds the genius type to logic except where fooling their quarry is concerned. A sight to shake up any self-respecting drinking man occurred last summer on a Texas lake I occasionally visit. Two men in a boat near ours had a six-pack of beer. Not on ice. Just sitting on the boat seat in the hot sun as they rigged their rods. Suddenly I saw one of them tear open the package and pop the top of the can. I didn't see how he could stand hot beer. And then I did a doubletake.

"Did you see *that?*" I asked my partner in astonishment. "He poured the beer over the side!"

This happened again in a moment, and after a bit both were casting. We couldn't resist. We moved in on them and asked what the pitch was.

"Oh," one said. "We don't drink the beer. We just wanted the shiny pop-top tabs. We put hooks on 'em. They wiggle. Great, man!"

My partner mulled this. At last he said, "I think we could form a good partnership, friend. You let me keep the beer on ice, and I'll guarantee to hand you a fresh tab any time you need one. I may even hand you a few extra!"

One of the sneakiest and by all odds the creepiest thing ever to befall a fish is the now overwhelmingly popular and productive plastic worm. These worms, as everyone knows, are authentic replicas, in soft, slithery plastic, of real worms. Just who made up the first one is not clear. But I do know that several seasons before these lures hit the world of angling like a bomb, an obscure tinkerer friend of mine molded some rather crude ones. He was not thinking about fish at the time. He made these, earthworm color and all, and hid a couple in a big bowl of cold salad at the home of a mutual friend where we were invited to dine. After the screaming, the nausea and mortification were all wound up, another guest got a scheming glint in his eye, pocketed the worms, and took off for the nearest pond.

I never heard what happened. But when the first plastic worms appeared on the market, in good old logical "worm color," I would have bet no self-respecting bass would touch one. Quite the contrary, bass started *eating* the cottonpickin' things. I have now on many occasions watched a bass actually take a big plastic worm into its mouth, gum it, and swallow it. Kind of sickening in a way. And not quite fair. But the plastic-worm gimmick didn't stop there. Devious schemers started asking for purple worms, baby-blue worms, bright-red worms, green worms. At first it was pretty darned kooky, believe me, to watch some fisherman grinning kind of foolishly to himself and stringing a purple worm on a hook. But they *worked*—all the colors worked—like crazy. It was a tossup whether man or bass was most wacky.

One recent season I was fishing a small lake and had with me a squinch-eyed fisherman who never ceases his search for the end-all killer. We were not catching anything. He saw in my tackle box some plastic worms in translucent gold. He grabbed at one quick as a cat.

"That's no good," I said.

"Then why do you carry it around?"

He had me.

191

"I got a plan," he said. There was a sudden almost psychotic look about him. "Bass have seen every other color, right? Who has showed 'em a gold worm? Nobody! Show 'em a gold worm!"

I showed 'em a gold worm. A big bass eased up and gaffered it like it was the last of its race and pure protein.

"You see—you see?" My buddy was ecstatic. "Gimmee one, quick!"

We sat there and caught bass until we were ashamed. When we were through this guy tucked the worms almost sadly back into my box. "I'm never going to try it again," he said. "I'm scared to death it wouldn't work—and that would really shake me."

Possibly the most curious segment of the world of fishing kooks, at least in my experience, is the fish smellers. Not that they smell *like* fish. No, they go out to *smell* fish. It sounds a little far out, I know. But there are these people. For example, I know an Alabama brim smeller. And I know another gentleman on the Texas coast who smells schools of certain saltwater fish. Think they're not dead serious? You ought to go out with one on a smelling expedition!

Shortly after I had heard of, and met, the Alabama brim smeller, two of us arranged for him to take us out. A brim (or bream), for those who may not know, is a sunfish, generally a bluegill. But in some parts of the South there are yellowbelly brim, redear brim—other species of sunfish. We were going out to smell a bedding ground of redear brim, better known to some anglers as shellcrackers.

The brim-smelling expert was a lank cracker with his eyes a little bit close together and a long, hawk-type nose. First thing he did when we met him at the dock was to smell us. "I'd sorta like to have you wash under your arms," he said apologetically.

It raised my hackles. "I did wash," I said.

192

"Yeah, but you got some of that smelly stuff on. It bothers my nose."

We took off our shirts and washed the Left Guard into the lake. We got into the boat and Lanky started along the shore of a big, swampy area. He explained: "This time a' year the redear brim start beddin'. Big rafts of 'em swarm around and make beds and lay their aigs in the shallers. Causes a lot of stirrin'. Fellers that knows what to smell fer can smell 'em."

He slowed here and there. My friend started to light a cigarette. "Don't smoke, please sir," Lanky said. "Confusin' to my nose."

Now we drifted, close in. Lanky was standing — sniff, sniff, sniff — heading the boat just so into a very small breeze — sniff, sniff.

"A few yonder," he said. "Not many."

Such nonsense, I thought. Reminded me of the old guide feeling the game track and telling instantly just how many hours old it is. Good show! But a little later old Lanky allowed we were getting close to the main bunch. We had foxed him on one thing. We knew he hadn't had anything pre-located here, for we were staying near this dock and he lived a good many miles away and hadn't been near here.

At last he eased in, let an anchor down very gently. "They's a passel of 'em all over year," he announced. "Go t'fishin'."

We did. And we murdered the redear brim. I even began to believe *I* could smell the odor he tried to explain to us. And I am convinced, having seen this done elsewhere, and with friends who have seen it accomplished by a Texas-coast fish smeller out in open blue water, that it is no hoax. In fact, numerous Texas saltwater hands look for "slicks" caused by schools of trout feeding and then regurgitating portions of their chopped-up forage. They get downwind from these slicks and sniff around, claiming a watermelon-like smell is what they are seeking. Kooks these guys may be, but if so they're expert ones and they eat fish often.

That gets us to the marshmallows, and I really hate to even think about that. On my first visit to Hebgen Lake near West Yellowstone, Montana, a few years ago I spent most of a day wading along a deserted stretch of shoreline, trying in vain to catch some of the trout I had been assured were here in swarms. I had changed spoons until I was on the third time around for my whole collection. About then I rounded a point where a road came close to shore. Lined along the beach were dozens of fishermen, and women, too. Most had brought along camp stools and lawn chairs. Here in talkative comfort they lounged, like a gathering at a shuffleboard court in a development for retirees. With great curiosity, I approached to have a look. It was surely a pleasant way for a lot of tourists to dawdle in their time. They didn't need to catch anything. They had each other. Then my cozy tolerance changed to astonishment. I saw several rod tips bobbing, several other persons on down the beach landing trout. And finally, at close range, as I walked down the line, I was seeing string after string of trout lying in the water.

"How are you catching those?" I asked one man. I'm sure I sounded incredulous.

"Why," he said, as if amazed that I didn't know, "marshmallows, of course. What else?"

I thought he was pulling my leg. With sarcasm I said, "Tell me, what *color* do you think is best?"

"Pink," he said. "Beats white all to hell. Here—try one."

It was true. Marshmallows had caught all those trout. They do it every summer, there and elsewhere. Crazy? Like a vision. Spelled nightmare. But, like the feller said, it ain't easy to argue with success!

194

17
Catching Trout in the West

There is a certain small, high-country lake in western Montana that is one of the most delightful cutthroat trout waters I know. The trout are not really large — 14 or 15 inches is about average maximum. The reason I like the place so much is that the trout and I agree on how they must be caught. This is a most peculiar, individual piece of water, and during the weeks of summer at least, only one method is consistently successful.

My family and I camped there one year. As I was cleaning trout for an evening meal I watched a most exasperated individual work his way up the lakeshore toward me. He had been fishing most of the day. I'd seen him catch only one trout. Now he approached and paused, looking at my limit.

"I don't understand it," he said. "I've worn out every

spoon and spinner, large and small, that I own, along with my arm. One measly trout!"

I very much dislike the feeling of having been successful when someone else has not. I said, "Can you fly-fish at all?"

"I've an outfit," he replied. "I'm not very good."

I dug out several dry flies that were made with closed-cell sponge-rubber bodies. These flies, excellent mayfly replicas, made beautifully by a small firm in Land O'Lakes, Wisconsin, originally as bluegill flies, don't soak up and sink. That is a tremendous advantage for lake fishing—and for dubs.

"You don't have to be good," I told him. "Use this leader—here. It is fine. That's the main thing. Get one of these small gray flies out there any old way you can and just let it lie. Still-fish with it. But watch closely. Suddenly a cruising trout will knife from below and gobble it. You have to be quick setting the hook."

"Don't I move it?"

"Let it lie until line disturbance settles. Then if you wish, creep it a few inches, let it lie again. The creep is simply to call attention."

He went to his camp thankful but not convinced. Next midmorning he was back, beaming. He had filled his limit.

This gentleman was from the Great Lakes region, a summer visitor to the West. Thousands of fishermen from the East, Midwest and South converge annually upon the mountain West. Many have fished for trout. Many are only so-so trout fishermen. A few are darned good—at home. They, and others with no trout experience, have been primed with glowing accounts of Western mountain trout fishing. All are eager to try. These visitors envision a trout fisherman's paradise where all they have to do is give the trout a chance to get caught.

The sad fact is, it doesn't work that way. Not more than

10 percent who live outside the mountain West and visit there for summer vacations do well with trout fishing. Many quite expert trouters fail because they try to fish as they fish at home. That is the hurdle. Trout, as all anglers know, can be difficult, regardless of where. But Western high-country trout fishing differs drastically from elsewhere.

I was brought up fishing trout in the Great Lakes area. On my first Western venture I was excited, eager—and totally lost. The waters, compared to what I was used to, were so different. What I'd called a river at home was a creek. What Westerners called a creek often turned out to be a brawling river in which one could stand up and drink. I saw lakes swarming with trout I could not catch. I saw wild torrential streams I did not believe trout could live in—until I watched some native, or blooded visitor, snake 'em out by the sackful. After a few trips I learned that if I wanted to catch trout in the West I had to start over. This *was* different. Myriad influences upon the trout were different. Some of it, I learned—slowly, the hard way—and herewith pass on.

That little dry-fly lake in Montana. . . . At high altitudes, trout food is scarce. It is also, by standards elsewhere, extremely limited in *variety*. At first this is perplexing. Especially with spinning so popular nowadays, a majority will automatically start hurling spoons or spinners. In some places these will work just fine. But in a lake like this, which as it happens has no other fish in it—no forage species—trout are not used to eating anything comparable in appearance. The flash of a spoon may be meaningless.

I had thought first, here, in terms of fly-fishing with nymphs, sunk well down. Sometimes those trout *must* feed on nymphs. But I didn't catch trout. At least twice a day, however, the surface swarmed with rising trout, taking winged insects. I used an Adams dry-fly pattern of modest

197

Many Western streams, like the Firehole shown here, may have shallow runs, but they also have many very deep holes.

On many large rivers such as the famed Madison, fishing wet flies or bait upstream is deadly.

size. Trout took it. I switched to a closed-cell sponge rubber body because of its excellent buoyancy. It did fine. I visited that lake several times over several seasons. Invariably, dry-fly fishing was the *only* way to catch trout there in summer.

This, mind you, might not work elsewhere, even on a lake maybe just over the ridge. That is one of the first principles of Western trout fishing. Each water is inclined to be extremely individual. You must forget what you know, ferret out what to do *here*. In high lakes particularly, available food is the key. Trout diet in these waters is monotonous. That makes your problem a pinpoint one, but it can be solved if you are determined.

Most of the famed Western trout rivers confuse visitors because of their large size. They are also more difficult to read. Some, like the Madison, just upstream inside Yellowstone Park, offer long stretches that appear to have little trout cover. Yet some great trout live here. How do you find them? Think of cover not as what you may call trout cover at home — an old snag, a sunken log, a big bank undercut far back by a deep hole. There are hundreds of small pockets along the smooth, low bank of the Madison in this stretch that you would not look twice at back home. The river is so broad the undercut pockets seem miniatures. But many hold good trout. These pockets, in this piece of river, are the most important cover. Trout have learned how to live here by taking advantage of them.

Even visiting fishermen already informed of this do not always succeed. Once I watched a very good caster laying dry flies along such a bank. He did take an occasional trout. But trout hiding under a low bank like this are not there to take surface material. They do that out in the current. You must cast from out in the stream *toward* the bank. Not several feet from it, but exactly *against* it. Your fly must be wet, and sink quickly. Thus it passes low and in sight in front of a trout in its lair. I've watched the late Paul Young, Sr. of Laredo, Texas, who was one of the finest trout fishermen I knew, spend two hours fishing one short stretch of bank as described, on the Madison, taking and releasing as many as a dozen trout in the 3-pound category!

There is a further angle which has to do with types of flies. I've watched many trouters open a fly box and bullheadedly use stuff they'd use at home. True, many flies will catch trout anywhere. But you just can't beat listening to and copying the "Romans." A classic example is the tremendous play the Woolly Worm and its imitations and variations get in the West. Some, hackles and all, are a half-inch in diameter, tied on a long-shanked hook almost as long as your thumb. I've watched many a visitor look with surprise and contempt upon these ungainly "bugs." When cast, they make a splatt like a cork bass bug. Then they sink and drift along, looking far too large for any trout to take. But I've hauled many a trout from under a bank with just such a weird conglomeration. Numerous large nymphs live in these streams. Thus the success of the imitations.

This gets us to what "large" *really* means in terms of Western trout rivers. In addition to the flat, modestly shallow runs, all large streams have very big, very deep holes. Even streams of medium size, like the Firehole, have tremendous holes. Trout in most of these rivers lie deep. Only a few Western waters are truly good dry-fly streams. Most are too fast for comfortable dry-fly fishing, and often too rough. In addition, trout here are schooled to deep feeding. The average visiting fly-fisherman never gets his wet fly deep enough. And, though he may be very successful fishing streamers back home, he finds them in most Western streams not as effective as other wets because of lack of small fishes they imitate. Nymphs, large and small — which a majority of trout anglers fish least expertly of all fly lures — are far and away the most successful sunken flies in the West.

200

However, to get them deep enough requires help. Here the sinking fly line is a must. There are varieties available that sink swiftly, slowly, or with a length of tip that sinks while the remainder floats. A most interesting experiment Paul Young and I did one season was to fish the same large Western stream day after day, switching off with: standard wet fly line; sinking line; sinking line with tiny split shot on the leader 18 inches above the fly. The last, though an abomination to cast, outcaught the other two double. The sinking line alone *tripled* the catch of the standard wet-fly line. It was all a matter of getting deep.

These large rivers are not only broad and deep, but deceptively swift. Tremendous currents seethe through their most placid-looking stretches—compared to what most trouters know back home. I recall how, in Michigan, I used to cast a wet fly or nymph to the bank, let it drift slowly around. This standard procedure worked well in many streams there because currents were modest. Not until I started fishing the West years ago did I see anglers commonly fishing wet flies, and bait with both fly and other rods, *upstream.* It is a lethal idea particularly adapted to the West.

The reason is that many of these large streams have small stones and gravel along the bottom. Some of course do contain huge boulders. But, again using the Madison as an example because it is well known, long stretches can be fished upstream because the strong current and lack of obstructions allow a nymph or other sunken fly to drift naturally. Back home it might continually sink to bottom and hang up. Not here. This is the perfect way to fish the nymph.

I've even caught trout in certain stretches by casting upstream and across, then wading along with my line, mending as I go. After a downstream walk I'd climb out, go back up, do it again. A lot of bother? Indeed. But deadly. Big, swift water took the fly too fast otherwise, pulled line, made the float unnatural. Bait, fished on a spin rod upstream by this method, simply cast upstream with no sinker or split shot and allowed to tumble back, while the rod is held high and slack line is kept reeled in, is murder. Spoons can be fished just as efficiently this way, tumbling and flashing. Yet, at home it is most difficult to do so because of smaller waters, sluggish currents, bottom obstructions.

The Gallatin River, between West Yellowstone and Bozeman, flows beside the highway many miles and is a classic example in many stretches of the boulder-strewn river that seems to roar and rant so wildly no trout could possibly live there. A truly experienced fisherman — whether with flies, bait or lures — would recognize the potential in these stretches. The average visitor is not always that experienced. I well recall my first look here, where big boulders are scattered and at first glance it appears to be a jumble of whitewater torrents.

Where would trout be, if indeed anywhere here? I learned where: on the lower side of each big current-breaking boulder. But some of these pockets are so small — a square yard of gin-clear slack — and so confusing to look at because of cross currents and eddies that a first-timer would pass it up as useless. Indeed, I've watched tourists stop along here, a couple of fishermen make a few casts just any old place in the river, shake their heads and go on. *But,* by fishing *exactly* to those small slicks behind the boulders, a limit of good trout can be caught in a hurry, with wet fly, worm, or spinner. Sometimes you get only a split-second float through a Gallatin glide. Current tears at your line, whipping the lure away. But bear in mind, these trout live here, under these specific conditions. They're conditioned to darting swiftly at any food ripping across their tiny bailiwicks. It's one more lesson a visitor should learn.

Under the conditions above, pinpoint casts are mandatory. On average large Western trout rivers—I picture the upper Missouri, the Yaak, Flathead, Blackfoot, many others—the fisherman used to making puny casts may be lost. The short cast may be most successful at home on a stream 30 to 50 feet wide. Here, because of wading difficulties, much of the best water cannot be reached unless you really push out line. Long floats are often needed. In spinning, using spoons, you must reach the edge of a current rip that cannot be fished properly without plenty of line out.

Long casts aren't difficult in spinning. But in fly-casting, "reach" requires special equipment: powerful rod, forward-taper line or one of the modern short fly lines backed by monofil, or else by a very light, slender, flat (level) extra length of special fly line. You may have to go to a fly reel of larger capacity. If you are after large trout in big water you most certainly will want plenty of backing on any fly reel.

In summer, many Western streams fall swiftly. Moss grows in them far worse than in most streams elsewhere. It becomes a real problem. Dry flies in this low, very clear water are extremely difficult. Wet flies are practically mandatory. This is where the floating line with a short sinking tip greatly assists the wet-fly man. Oddly, few of these excellent lines are used because fishermen just do not realize their potential to lick low clear water and the moss problem.

There are trout anglers who've fished a lifetime without ever using either felt-soled waders or wading staff. They never needed them. Yet many a Western trout-fishing vacation has been ruined for lack of these. Invariably in Western streams both are "must" equipment, especially the felt soles. Western streams can be exceedingly dangerous without them. Better even than felt-soled waders, which wear out quickly because no wader maker to my knowledge has ever built them thick enough, are the felt-soled slip-on sandals that buckle over the instep of one's waders.

Left: Streams like the Gallatin really roar and roll. Trout lie in small pockets below boulders. *Right:* High-country lakes are often difficult. Here in the San Juan Primitive Area of Colorado a guide showed me how to rack up cutthroats with small frog-finish spoons.

Facing page: Poor timing ruins many trips. It may be spring in Pennsylvania but in the Western high country snow may lie along stream banks and lakes may still be frozen.

Perhaps the largest contributor to disillusionment for visitors is *poor timing.* High-country weather isn't like any other. It may be spring in Pennsylvania, or summer, but lakes at 10,000 feet may still be frozen, and snowbanks may line rivers. If you do not check conditions exactly, you may get to the stream of your dreams to find it a roiling flood, so discolored from runoff that it is useless for fishing. Steep mountains and much snow make runoff a big problem in the West. But certain streams get far more than others. State fisheries men can straighten you out on the bad ones and the good ones.

Large streams to which other large streams are tributary take a long time to clear. The Snake, for example, gets an awesome amount of muddy water poured in from such big streams as the Gros Ventre. Don't ruin your chance by going too early. The period immediately following heavy run-

off, and prior to the lowered water of summer, is very good.
But what so few fishermen planning westward trips realize is
that early fall is often the very best time of all. In September
and early October the big influx of tourists has faded, the
streams are generally in good condition, and trout are really
on the prod.

Timing, of course, can have a good deal to do with trout
movements. You may hear, for example, that the Flathead
River is a great place to catch big Dolly Vardens. It is. But
only, at any given place, during a certain *period* of the
summer when the big bulls are moving upstream. They
spawn in fall, far up in headwaters. Once the main movement
has passed any given point, fishing can be virtually useless.
Water temperature moves trout, too. I think of Crystal
Creek, a lovely stream pouring into the Gros Ventre. Often
in summer hordes of big cutthroats push into the cold, clear

water of this stream because it is cooler than the Gros Ventre. This upstream movement has nothing to do with spawning. These trout spawn in spring. The same phenomenon occurs for short periods in many Western streams.

Or, there are the famed hatches like the so-called salmon-fly hatch on the lower Madison. You can't just make a run at such a bonanza without knowing what you're doing. It is a progressive thing, beginning far downstream and backing upstream day by day as weather and water warm. If your time is limited, you could go to the wrong part of the river, or arrive a few days early or late. A close check with state authorities or guides is mandatory if you wish to get in on such hot fishing.

The most basic advice of all is to put away your home prejudices and opinions and go West with an open mind, prepared to watch and listen to natives and others who evidence success. At a high lake in Wyoming I learned one summer from a native to just sit and wait out the dawn and early morning—a period when, at home, I'd have been into some of the day's best fishing. The reason? Chilly early hours saw little insect activity, and usually a flat lake surface. It was invariably midmorning before trout did any upper-water feeding. And by then as a rule a breeze had begun to riffle the surface. With the riffle, line and leader did not show blatantly, and trout were fairly easy to take. When the lake was flat they were just next to impossible.

Another time, preparing to make a horseback trip far into the San Juan Primitive Area in Colorado, the guide showed me a small box full of Dardevle spoons, about 1½ inches long, all of them frog finish. He smiled wisely.

"One lake we're going to," he said, "contains cuts mostly around a foot long. We'll camp there and will need to depend on them for several meals. So I want to be sure."

I don't suppose there was a frog within miles of that

lake. But for some reason the trout banged those spoons incessantly. To be sure, they also struck others, and flies as well. But not consistently. All we had to do at mealtime was rig with the frog finish, and spend about twenty minutes. Why did they strike? The guide didn't know either, nor did the same spoons do much in other lakes we tried.

One of my most vivid recollections relative to the necessity of keeping an open mind concerns a trip I made by 4WD over an awesomely rough trail to a timberline lake in northern New Mexico one fall. When we arrived, two other fishermen were there. The lake was small, and supposedly stiff with big cutthroats, fish of 3 or more pounds.

There was not a rise anywhere, which seemed logical this time of year. Timber grew so close to the water's edge that fly-casting was virtually impossible. My partner and I had brought both fly and spin tackle, and decided probably spoons would catch the big cuts. We made passing acquaintance with the strangers and glanced at how they were rigging up. It was obvious to us that these fellows must be flatlanders from the Midwest who were used to fishing for warmwater panfish. They were going to cast plastic bubbles, partly water-filled, with a couple of feet of line trailing and a nondescript panfish-type fly at its end.

It just so happened that while I had fly-fished for years for bluegills with a fly rod, I had never in my fishing life used spinning tackle and a bubble, for anything. And it was obvious to me that the big *splatt* of that bubble dropping would send every trout to the bottom. Certainly nothing would follow a fly that had a big blob of clear plastic bouncing and making a V swath ahead of it.

By now of course you are way ahead of me. Those fellows weren't from the plains. They were natives and they had been here before. Such splashing and wallowing of big trout! All we went down the mountain with was envy.

18
The Paddlefish:
Mystery Monster from Missouri

Chuck Purkett was directing operations. He had the motor throttled down just so and he was quartering attentively across a big bend of the murky, swollen Osage River near Warsaw, Missouri. For April, it was hot. Thunderheads were building and we'd heard that west of us tornado warnings were out.

A tornado, I reflected, couldn't do much with me. It was already done. For two solid hours I had clenched a big, stiff, heavy saltwater fishing rig with a line like a rope. As regularly and endlessly as my heartbeat, I'd give a heaving upward jerk on the rod. Jerk, let down, jerk, let down. At line's end was a conglomeration of junk — a fist-sized lead sinker, a couple of outsized treble hooks strung above it. This was ten years at hard labor!

"It wouldn't help even to be nuts," I croaked at Chuck. "Nor drunk. A drunk man would be scared to death he'd hook one of those monsters!"

We were fishing for paddlefish, which means snagging. Between mid-March and mid-May, the spring season in Missouri, if you don't go snagging for paddlefish you just don't have status. But by now I was beginning secretly to hope I'd go home smelling statusless. I was bushed and I knew if I lucked into one it would be a tough fight. I wasn't sure I had one left in me.

Chuck grinned. Chuck Purkett knows more about paddlefish than probably any other individual in the whole world. He discovered and identified the first free-floating paddlefish eggs, did likewise for the fry, and he was the first to successfully propagate paddlefish in a hatchery. This might not sound like much to the uninitiate, but once you've seen a paddlefish it does, because the critter is anything but believable.

Chuck cut the throttle and said, "What do you think of that one?"

A boat was bearing down along our port side, the two inhabitants jerking away like mechanical contraptions. They had a real old buster, maybe 50 or 60 pounds, tied alongside. I quit jerking and stared at it. The fish was as long as I was, and in the middle easily as big around. It had a great, broad and deeply forked tail that looked as if it could slap a man out of a boat. But that *face!* The snout continued on from the head in a fantastic spatula almost a yard long and two hands broad. At the base of this two gimlet eyes stared witlessly, and beneath and behind these a cavernous mouth was set, dressed off at the sides of the head by a pair of elongated gill flaps big enough to make loincloths for a Japanese wrestler.

"Crank her up, Chuck," I murmured. "It ain't real."

We chugged away, jerking, methodically covering the

Top: Paddlefish headquarters — Warsaw, Missouri. In town a huge replica honors this ancient fish. *Left:* What a mug and snout! The paddlefish is a curious creature indeed. *Right:* Bob Needham lifts my paddlefish by the bill, and I am really glad the battle is over.

210

big bend. Chuck, who is Chief of the Division of Fisheries for the Missouri Department of Conservation, had told me a lot about our astonishing quarry when I arrived the previous evening to try the snagging sport. Young Bob Needham, a biologist then working for Chuck doing some advanced paddlefish studies, had further filled me in.

"This is perhaps the most remarkable freshwater fish known to man," Bob had said. "It is literally 'old as the hills,' one of our most primitive fishes. Fossil forms have turned up from the ancient Eocene shales in Wyoming."

The paddlefish predates the bony fishes, hasn't a bone in its body. Just cartilaginous material. That great big mouth hasn't a sign of a tooth, either, and the jaws are in fact very weak. To make a living the fish strains plankton and small insect life out of the water through its big mug and gill chambers. In place of an authentic spinal column it has a primitive notochord.

The case history of the paddlefish is in fact one amazement after another. Called colloquially "spoonbill" or "spoonbill cat," it is not a catfish, nor even remotely related. It is in a family of its own, and there are only two species, the one living in bayous, large lowland streams and lakes of our Mississippi Valley and system, the other in the valley of the Yang-tse-Kiang, in China!

I had asked Bob Needham how large Osage River paddlefish averaged. "Anywhere from 20 to 70 pounds as a rule," he said. "One was taken here last year that weighed 78. A few have been caught somewhat larger."

I'd located old records from half a century ago, in Indiana: a fish from Lake Tippecanoe that was 6 feet 2 inches, 4 feet around, and 150 pounds, another from Lake Manitou at 163 pounds. They used to be a big-stuff commercial fish at that time, the Mississippi Valley producing as much as 2,000,000 pounds annually. Little ones were sneakily sold in

Southern markets, with heads, tails and fins lopped off, as "boneless cat."

Chuck had showed me a bushel-sized gob of paddlefish eggs, where one had been gutted. It looked like a shapeless mass of charcoal-colored sponge plastic. The individual eggs are extremely small. During the bygone commercial days along the Mississippi, an average 10,000 pounds a year of eggs went to make spoonbill caviar. I wondered what the gourmets' stomachs would have felt like had they seen the source!

Bob Needham had said, "Sometimes during heavy spawning runs, when there's a good rise on the river to bring a lot of fish out of Lake of the Ozarks all at once, they're so thick in the river outboarders actually shear pins on 'em."

Chuck Purkett and I didn't seem to be having that trouble right now. Then suddenly there was a wild roil of water right beside the boat.

"Big one rolling," Chuck said. He quickly maneuvered the boat. "Might be more."

He got it turned so that my rig would pass through the area. They roll on the surface occasionally during spawning runs, but they do most of their swimming and feeding close to bottom. You have to keep the snag hooks down there. It's best, I'd been told, if you feel bottom each time you let back.

There! I had one! Damn, I was into a brute. I could not hold the rod. I yelled at Chuck, "Shut her down!"

He did. I fought the monster mightily for several minutes. We drifted below. Chuck said, "It doesn't seem to move."

"It's so cussed big it doesn't know I've got it," I said, wildly excited. I guess I had some fight left in me after all. I gave a powerful heave.

Chuck said gently, "I'm afraid you're hung into a log on bottom."

212

He eased up into position and angled in from where we'd drifted. We worked away at the mess. Finally it came loose. Silently I hauled up and cleaned the hooks. They were 9/0 trebles. I tested the points. Plenty sharp. The hide of a paddlefish is tough. I got the 12-ounce sinker unwound so it dangled properly at line's end. The hooks were spaced about 15 inches apart up the line above.

"Well," I told Chuck sheepishly, "it was a pretty good thrill, anyway. Let's give it the old heart-attack special once more." Presently I was sweatily jerking my way upriver again.

It's the spawning urge in paddlefish that sends them up the rivers seeking likely spots, and that makes the sport of spoonbill snagging possible. And it occurs in many places besides Warsaw, Missouri, including several spots in the Dakotas. But over the years one of the most important paddlefish fisheries has been out of Lake of the Ozarks, with Warsaw and Osceola both hotspots, partly because of proximity to the big lake, and partly because there are many virtually perfect spawning grounds in the Osage and one or two tributaries.

Next morning Chuck and I made a run by car some miles to the confluence of the Pomme de Terre River and the Osage, while Marvin Bybee, a friend of Chuck's, graciously made the trip by boat so we'd be all set to fish without the long boat ride. This confluence and its consequent deep holes and swirls was an especially fiery spot for paddle-fishermen. I was glad to get a chance alone with Chuck, for I'd been trying to pry from him some of the facts on which his fame among ichthyologists was based, and Chuck is a very modest gent.

We hit the Pomme de Terre dock just as Bybee rounded the bend below. We also hit it just as a pair of snaggers were coming in. They had four great fish—two per snagger is a limit—tied alongside. My eyes bugged. It is common practice to snub the fish to the boat rather than attempting to take them aboard. But four all at once—I'd seen nothing like this. All were in the 50-pound class.

I said to the gent at the motor, "How long you boys been out—since Christmas?"

He grinned. "About three hours. The one there"—he pointed to the largest—"gave us a real tangle."

Chuck said, "You see, it *can* happen."

We got into the boat and started right in. "You never know," Chuck said. "Might hit one here—anywhere. The thing is, though, the old hands get so they know the kind of a hole paddlefish like best, and they don't fool with other places. Year after year, these holes pay off." After a few minutes of jerking we reeled up and headed for a hole Chuck had in mind, and I got him launched on his story.

The ugly old spoonbill, it seems, is a far more important resource than most people realize. In addition to the recreational values, lots of people like the flesh, after a fish is properly cleaned and the fat along the sides cut away. Though many other anglers may prefer to fish for bass or trout, the fact remains that spoonbill-snagging season, with April usually the peak month, has for years drawn an astonishing crowd to the Osage River. As an example, one season canvas a few years ago showed upwards of 23,000 snaggers taking a jerk at it here, and an awesome 8,200 fish recorded, with a gross weight of 107 tons! There is also a fall season, but it's nowhere near as productive.

Reflecting on such figures for several years, and upon the fact that nobody really knew anything much about the paddlefish, in Missouri or elsewhere, Chuck Purkett decided somebody had better find out. Tantalizing was the fact that nobody had any idea what a fresh-hatched paddlefish looked like. Many infant fish of various species bear little resemblance to the adults. And intriguing in past years had been

214

the standing offer made by Mr. Allis, of Allis Chalmers, of a cool $1,000,000 cash for a spoonbill under 2 inches long. Had Mr. Allis known Chuck Purkett, with Purkett's dedicated determination to fill this ichthyological gap, it's a cinch he'd not have slept well.

As it was, the loot was never claimed. One scientist team did finally find some baby spoonbills about an inch long, but too late to cash in. But still no one had any idea of exact spawning areas, or had ever found deposited eggs, or newly hatched fry. For a full century the search by numerous leading fisheries men had dragged fruitlessly on—until Chuck wrote in his diary on April 24, 1960, "A day to remember!"

Chuck told me, "Years ago scientists weren't concerned with paddlefish conservation. But this fish is a kind of a lost chord in the train of evolution and it was felt a study of its life beginnings might help fill in the facts. However, my reason was mainly to try to save the paddlefish from near extinction."

Purkett went at his chore like a regular detective. He sleuthed through hundreds of snaggers, asking questions, studying every known and imaginative angle. Obviously the reason the fish ran up this and other rivers was that they desired certain spawning conditions not found in lakes. Current was undoubtedly one. Probably rock or gravel not covered by silt, as in the lake, might be another.

"In 1958 we got spawn and milt from fish snagged near Osceola," Chuck said, "and I had my eye on the spot as an actual spawning site."

He tried valiantly to hatch some of the spawn, and he failed. He began hearing from fishermen of fish activity that suggested to him something to do with spawning. But the next year low water kept most of the fish from running the river. He was stalled.

The following spring, however, about the time the water

hit the required 50 degrees, there was a big rise on the river. Chuck suspected fish were swarming in. They could now easily cross the bars. Then as the water eased down he started seeing rolling fish near the mouth of Weaubleau Creek. There were gravel bars here.

"A fish would come to the surface," he explained, "slosh its tail, and disappear. I suspected it might mean a female was rushing up from the gravel, dispersing eggs en route by the tail sloshing. Pursuing males could be releasing milt as eggs settled. But I was just guessing."

However, the precise activity continued all afternoon and evening and Chuck's curiosity was really aroused. "I felt I was on the verge of something," he told me. "I had spent endless days and nights on the river, listening, watching, poking around. It's a big place—and I didn't know exactly what I was looking for."

Again they managed to get eggs and milt, and desperately tried to hatch them. It was no go. But meanwhile Chuck did find out a little about what the fertilized eggs looked like. And then came the big day.

"It didn't look like it," Chuck said, grinning wryly. "The water suddenly dropped sharply. It went down seven feet. The gravel bars where I'd suspected spawning were partially exposed. Then lightning struck—I walked along a bar and right away spied a tiny egg. Boy, this was something! I picked it up feeling like I'd struck gold—and my hands shook so I dropped it into the water!"

Now he frantically began searching. And a great relief swept him. The quick drop of the river actually had been a real godsend. The water a bit downstream in small pools was full of eggs, hatching eggs, and tiny fish not more than a couple of hours old. Ichthyological history and Chuck Purkett had collided head-on, and presently with assistants he had collected everything in sight and was exultantly headed

216

back to the lab, ready this time to successfully propagate paddlefish.

"Weren't you thinking a little wistfully of Mr. Allis?" I asked with a grin.

At that very instant I hit a fish. A thrill shot through me the likes of which I never thought I could experience at this game. There was a whoosh of line and Chuck hit the throttle to shut us down. It was over as quickly as it started. Of all the lousy luck. The brute was gone, and so was a goodly supply of my adrenalin. I was weak all over.

Chuck said, "Funny. Usually once you get a hook in, it stays. Maybe you ought to heave a little harder and sharper, just in case." I tried to wither him with a look but he just grinned.

The next day Chuck had to go back to his Jefferson City office. Bob Needham had seven big female paddlefish tied up by their tails to buoys out in the river, and he was giving them daily hormone shots in a spawning experiment they were running. "As soon as I doctor my fish," he told me, "I'll meet you and we'll try the river near Warsaw. I just feel you're in for a lucky streak by now."

I stood on a dock and watched six early birds in a row bringing in fish. They didn't seem to think there was anything to it. One pair had got two fish from the same hole, hooked in the first quarter-hour away from dock. They were still glowing from the fight. By the time Needham had jabbed his old lassoed girls I had a full head of steam up and my neck was really bowed.

As we made our way up the river, in and out among slow-moving snaggers, Bob filled in a few more details of the Purkett story. By close study Chuck and his men found out that as the female fish releases her eggs they drift free, but the minute they're fertilized by the pursuing male, they become very adhesive. Each egg sticks to the first object it

217

touches. Clean gravel bars were the places where most of the eggs that stuck would hatch. Otherwise they'd be covered with silt.

"One reason we need to know all we can," Bob said as he paused and we got our snagging apparatus ready, "is that there are plans to build a reservoir at Warsaw that will cut off the Osage. It's our best paddlefish stream."

Chuck had informed me that because of dam building during late years, there are very few adequate paddlefish facilities left anywhere in their range and it just could be that this ancient gaffer is doomed unless someone sticks up for it. The Mississippi River, which used to be a tremendous paddlefish haven, is about ruined for them because of the building of navigation pools.

"They have few spawning sites, now," Chuck had said, "and they have dropped to a precarious low—they're down about 90 percent from what they were at turn of the century."

"We hope," Bob said with a grunt as he heaved out his rig, "that when the new reservoir is built here at Warsaw provisions can be made to protect the fish and their spawning sites. Otherwise we're going to lose one of the most interesting and unusual fishing sports in the Ozarks."

Several years later I was to hear from Chuck Purkett that the paddlefish were indeed in difficulty. Construction of Harry Truman Dam had begun at Warsaw and it was obvious its completion would cut off the fish from their spawning areas, the gravel bars in the Osage River. A suit had been brought by the Environmental Defense Fund to halt the project. This delayed construction, but the Corps of Engineers, as all conservationists know, is a tough adversary. It was a foregone conclusion that by the middle 1970s the dam would be in place.

But Chuck was still going strong nonetheless. A three-year study had been launched, financed by the Corps, its purpose to further determine paddlefish cultural methods, to meticulously study also the tributaries of the Reservoir, such as the Sac, to find out if the fish might somehow utilize them.

"However," Chuck wrote, "the possible tributary streams are awfully small, so spawning success, if any, will be limited. And we'll still need wild brood stock from which to take eggs and milt for hatchery purposes. Without question the total number of fish will be drastically reduced regardless, once the dam is completed."

On that morning with Bob Needham, however, things were not looking so bleak. Even though I had not caught a fish so far, and had worked myself to a frazzle, I still found the whole procedure intriguing and I was ready for a fresh start, another round. The fantastic appearance of the fish made it all the more desirable as a trophy. We eased slowly up the river, Bob three-handed busy trying to manipulate his rig and run the boat. Suddenly, on a bend where a small tributary came in, a fish rolled near us. Immediately afterward Bob hit one—just bumping it with his sinker.

Excitement now buzzed in the boat like a swarm of bees. My arms were instantly less tired. I had forgotten how muggy and hot it was, and I found myself sitting tensely, heaving away with all my might. The river here was 200 or 300 feet wide. It occurred to me that this was Las Vegas fishing—you put down your dough and guess where the wheel will stop. Some skill and a good bit of knowledge is certainly handy. But mostly it's a straight gamble. How in the heck a fellow could hit a fish in all that water, even with those big hooks, I couldn't imagine.

"It's no sport for pessimists," I said to Bob.

Then, like that, it had happened. There was a jolt that loosened up my shoulder sockets. The rod groaned down.

"Log," I said. "I'm hung."

Bob cut the motor. He started reeling in fast. At that moment I couldn't tell if the boat had started its drift or if the log had moved off. Line direction changed. Like a clunk over the head with a club I suddenly knew for certain. We were drifting down toward where I'd hung, but still my rod was bowed. I had on all the pressure my muscles could dredge up, and still line was leaving the reel in a steady, inexorable movement that I knew I could not stop.

"Log, hell!" I yelled. I tried impulsively to stand up. The fish chose that moment to make a dash. It jerked me forward and almost overboard.

Bob said, "We'll have to go with it. It's a big one." He cranked up.

I now gained back a few turns. Then more, and more. We were bearing down on the fish. But Bob kept discreet distance so as not to foul the line. The brute was going with the current and we now just tagged along. But I suddenly realized that we had swung around. Bob had the motor turning very slowly, upstream, and still we were going down.

"Have we got this cussed thing," I gasped, "or has it got us?"

Bob chuckled. "Settle down," he said. "You've got a good long haul ahead of you."

As the fight went on the fish turned back and headed at a nice easy pace upstream. Then it made a spurt. I frantically took up line. The fish was passing us, and as the hook bit again to the snugging line, we saw it. It was just below surface and looked like a baby submarine.

"Great gods," I said. "I guess I'll just throw the rod overboard."

The monster surfaced then, gave a mighty roll and splash, and hit for the opposite bank. As we wore on and on with it, I was reminded of when I was in college and was on the wrestling team. University-style wrestling never did draw

220

a spectator crowd to amount to anything. It was unspectacular because though a pair of opponents might be straining every muscle, it didn't look like much. Only the fellow who'd done it knew what was going on, and inside him it was pretty darned dramatic.

But by the end of nearly half an hour a lot of the drama had gone and I was beginning to wish we could get the ancient critter corralled. We had now had several close-up looks. The fish was hooked well up toward the head, atop the back. That was good for the fish but not for us. It was not hurt, and it was in perfect position to use all its power to best advantage while not wearing down very fast. At last, however, we got it up near the boat and Bob took a long, careful look.

"I'll see if I can get it," he said. "Keep your line tight but be ready to let go. I don't want to get those hooks in me."

Bob had handled scores of paddlefish during his studies. He knew exactly how to seize the snout or the mouth and gill. But this time when he made his play, the fish exploded. Bob jumped back and I let the wild devil go. For another few minutes now I put on all the pressure possible. The fish now stayed on top. It was wearing thin. We figured it was upwards of 60 pounds.

When we made our next try, it was flapping weakly on its side, beaten. Bob Needham did a masterful job, while another boat watched from the sidelines. The fish was utterly exhausted, and he even brought it aboard, staying expertly clear of the hooks.

We sat and panted and grinned at each other and at the prize. Finally Bob said, "Well, the limit's two. You want to try for another?"

"I've been to Missouri and I've been shown," I said. "One monster is enough for me."

19

The Most Diminutive Salmon

There was a solid bump on my lure, and I snugged up and watched in wonder as the line with its lengths of varied colors rose higher and higher in the water, straightening. Then a beautifully streamlined platinum-hued fish shot out of the water and appeared to do a kind of aerial pirouette while enclosed in a sphere of exploding droplets.

I turned to Bill Browning and I also exploded. "It works!"

Browning was deaf, all tied up in a bit of business of his own. He had cut the motor from its trolling speed at my strike, and at that instant his rod tip had beckoned. I saw his stocky little shard of silver pop out back there where mine had just fallen, and I hurried now to get my line at a different angle, out of his way.

When you make your living chasing around the country

after fish and fish stories, you hear a lot of things. You get after a while so 99 percent of it slips right through the hole in your head. People are always hatching tall tales about fish and fishing methods and fishermen, and of course you never expect one to be true. It's a real thrill when one pans out.

Up near West Glacier, Montana, I had been fishing with Browning and he had remarked casually: "There's a fellow down at Lake Mary Ronan who, I've heard, has a real hex on kokanee. You know how tough they can be — and besides, nobody's ever made a real game fish of them until this came along. That's what I hear. We ought to drive over there."

The kokanee, as many anglers may know, is a land-locked miniature form of the sockeye salmon native to Idaho, Oregon, Washington, and British Columbia. This is the little salmon — smallest of the salmons — that has served for some years in Lake Pend Oreille, Idaho, and elsewhere, as food for Kamloops trout. It is supposedly solely responsible, because of its richness, for the amazing growth of these fish. But the kokanee has long been more than just that. Although at maximum it is only 12 to 15 inches and about 1 to 2 pounds, it is without question the most delicious of any fish ever invented. It has been stocked now in many of the Western states — Montana, California, Colorado, Wyoming, Nevada, Utah — even in New England and the Midwest. It has become a very popular quarry.

Nonetheless, I was not too enthused over Browning's announcement, for the one great trouble with the kokanee, from a true sport fisherman's point of view, is that catching it has long been an erratic business. It feeds mainly on plankton strained through its gill rakers. Lures have there-fore always been a problem. Besides, the methods used so far, I knew, so inhibited the fish that it couldn't do much when hooked except come obediently in.

"This man," Browning said, "has some mumbo-jumbo

223

mathematical approach, I've heard. He trolls, but with no weight, none of that string-of-cowbells junk. They say the fish leap like crazy."

That did it. I perked up my ears and next day we were easing down U.S. 93 south from Kalispell, drinking in the stunning views out over vast Flathead Lake. About halfway down Flathead, we found the gravel turn-off leading west to Lake Mary Ronan. A few minutes later, at the fishing resort he operated on the shore of this lovely spread of water, we met Bill Bringhurst, the kokanee genius.

Bringhurst, we were to learn, was just that, too. People were coming in off the lake. Everybody had limits. Each one we spoke to was a Bringhurst convert. We were told he'd made hundreds of them since he took over this place.

"The kokanee," he told us as we hurried down to his dock to get our first lesson, "is the bread-and-butter fish all through this country. It's tremendously abundant, you know. When the rainbows and all the other species won't hit, we'd go broke if we didn't have it to fall back on."

What had bothered Bill Bringhurst when he first came here, however, was that his "bread-and-butter" didn't always cooperate either. If he could just find some way to clobber kokanee surefire, he could keep his scores of guests satisfied regardless of weather, and doldrums in the other game-fish categories.

"People are happy," he told us, "if they are catching *something,* and most of them get so they don't fish anything else once they catch on to this method. They just have too much fun with the kokanee."

We already knew how a lot of people catch them sure-fire. They grind up crayfish or other chum and dump it on bottom, then fish over it with kernels of corn, or they jig small lures. The trouble is, chumming's not legal in Montana. Bringhurst didn't want any part of that. I recalled watching

224

people elsewhere troll quite successfully for kokanee with "cowbells." This fish stays rather deep a good share of the time. Those 4-foot-long strings of spinner blades in sizes diminishing from about like a man's palm on down through maybe a dozen to a small one at the end get down to the fish, all right. But I wouldn't give you a pewter quarter for that kind of fishing. You have to stop the boat to reel up or else you practically pull the motor backwards. And you have to reel up periodically to see if you've got a fish!

I told Bill Bringhurst this. He said, "My whole idea was to avoid that. Trolling, to be sure, lacks the action of casting. But it's a method everybody can use. I knew that an unhampered kokanee was the fightin'est little giant ever, with lots of jumps in him. If I could get him hooked on a free line, I was betting it would triple my business."

As he rigged tackle for us, he told us of the months he had spent on the lake, fiddling, trial and error, until he finally hit it. He handed Browning and me each a 6½-foot long-butted rod just sturdy enough to stay straight when trolling,

Left: Bill Bringhurst shows precisely how the rod must be set so line color segments ride just right. *Right:* These little salmon are handsome, silvery fish, and unbeatable on the table.

but with enough give to make playing even a small fish plenty of sport. On each rod was a Penn 109 level-wind reel suited to monofil. Other kinds can be used, of course. But this is the size and type Bringhurst used.

The line was what had us instantly curious. It was light lead-core line, a different color every 5 yards. Those colors, I was soon to understand, were the secret of Bill Bringhurst's unique system. I could see red, green, yellow, gray, blue and others on my reel. At line's end was a long monofil leader of 6- or 8-pound test.

"The level-wind reel is critical," he said. "Keeps the lead-core line from piling up. You have to watch that."

Leaders, he explained, could be 20 feet or so, along into the season, when the fish lie fairly deep. But early in season when they're at 10 to 15 feet only, he sometimes used one as much as 60 feet. Bringhurst claims that as the season progresses, the fact that the sun gets higher is actually what drives the fish deeper. He tied a small plastic lure at the end of each leader. The lures were all but weightless. A hooked fish thus would have almost no weight to battle. He led us to a boat and got us settled.

"Now don't ask a lot of foolish questions," he said. "You're going to think this sounds like some kind of witchcraft or pure nonsense. But just get out of your head all the preconceived ideas you may have about it, and do *precisely* as I tell you."

I wondered why a fish that strains plankton and water fleas through its gills would hit these tiny lures. I asked Bill Bringhurst and he told me all he knew was that they did, and that was good enough for him. He tapped a nail into the gunwale of the skiff on each side, set the rods against these with each rod butt against the opposite side of the boat. He carefully positioned the rods. Then he stood back and squinted.

226

"Rod tips exactly a yard above the water," he said. "They have to stay there, *exactly,* at all times."

That was where he lost me. I can take on so much and swallow it. But this old cynic wasn't going to lap up that much malarkey. We listened through the rest of it, however, and I was sure Bringhurst knew by then we weren't whole-heartedly buying it. It was just too pat.

Finally we were away. I grinned at Browning. We began to let out line exactly as Bringhurst had said. The idea was to troll, letting out, let's say, "four colors" of line. Red was the color we selected for immediately underwater, and green the one just above the water. We'd been instructed to make sure the meeting point of the two colors above and below water stayed *exactly* at the surface. In other words, red and green joined at the point where the line entered the water.

Obviously the only way to keep it this way was by boat speed—unless we moved the rod tips, which we'd been com-manded not to do. Browning, at the motor, adjusted the con-trols just so. For a moment the green length dipped about 6 inches under. Browning speeded up a wee bit until it was exactly right. It was easy to understand that what we were really doing was controlling both speed and lure depth by this color hocus-pocus.

I leaned back with one foot holding the butt of my rod solidly. I grinned. "I don't believe a darned bit of it," I said. "Lord, I've been through spooky stuff like this from coast to coast. Next thing they'll have me wearing a sack of lucky roots around my neck!"

Browning smiled wryly. We trolled for fifteen minutes. Green and red stayed precisely joined at the surface. Every kokanee in the lake stayed precisely unjoined to our lures.

"All right," Browning said at last. "Let's try a different color. That's what the man said."

We reeled up green. This put the red-gray meeting point

at water level when the rod tips were properly propped. A bit of breeze rose. Red sagged a foot under. Browning gave us a bit more gas. When we turned with the wind, gray came out a foot. Browning cut our speed down some. After a time we changed again, this time going deeper, letting green down into the water. Fifteen minutes later—nothing.

Another boat came near. We sat up with a start. Each of the two occupants had a fish on. "Bet they're trolling those cussed cowbells," I said. At that moment a kokanee shot out of the water as if it intended to fly off over the pine-clad mountains. Then the other followed. No cowbells, obviously. A fisherman can hardly lift 'em, let alone a small fish.

Bill Browning looked at me and his eyes were bulging. "There's only one thing to do," he said resolutely. "Ask 'em! Go ahead."

Bringhurst had explained that the "password" hereabouts among his converts was, "How many colors you fishing?" The theory was that all the kokanee were at the same depth at the same time. Letting down or taking up one color would actually change depth way back at leader's end very little. But, Bringhurst claimed, kokanee were finicky about this.

I yelled across at the neighboring boat: "How many colors?"

"Six," one busy angler shouted. "They're pretty well down."

"Voodoo," I muttered. "But I'll have to try."

With six colors down, we made a slow circle, rod tips just so, yellow-blue now meeting exactly at the surface.

Almost immediately Browning snorted. "Weeds." Then, "Heck, no. A fish!"

"Right!" I jumped up, seizing my own rod and cranking away. I had one, too.

From here on we were caught up in some of the most

astonishing fishing I have ever ah'ed over. We took limits of kokanee. We caught and released more. Some of them go free anyway, on their leaps. Because this fish feeds very little except by straining out small organisms, it has an exceedingly weak lower jaw. The lures we were using were fitted with a single hook. Most fish, for reasons I don't know, are hooked in the lower. It slips out easily when a fish leaves the water in one of those sparkling leaps so typical of the species when unencumbered.

Bill and I were now enthused. We decided during this and following sessions to test the Bringhurst theory thoroughly. When we were getting fish, we'd drop down one or two colors. Right away we were out of business. Or, we'd pull up one or two. The same, zero. Again part of the time one of us would fish at one depth, the other higher or lower. Now of course it did occur at times that a fish or two would be caught at each depth. But by and large the method worked spookily well. To further test it, we'd troll faster, or slower, changing the focus point where line colors joined. Invariably our catches fell off, or ceased entirely.

The best part of the system we suddenly discovered we'd been overlooking. It is this: When you catch a fish, there isn't any guessing. You know exactly at what depth to catch another. And, at what *speed*. Let's say you shut the motor off, as we did, when a fish is hooked. You play in your fish, and then you wonder how the dickens to find the proper spot and speed again. Nothing to it. Prop the rod with its tip in the same place, let down the same number of colors, adjust the motor so the last underwater color joins at surface with the one above—and there you are. *Bango!*

The first evening Bringhurst showed us his method of preparing kokanee to eat. They are rather oily. He neatly filleted each one, then slipped a sharp, thin-bladed knife between skin and flesh and pushed forward from the tail,

229

Left: Kokanee takes to the air after being hooked by the unique method we learned. *Right:* Into the net. Even though it takes a big one to weigh 2 pounds, the kokanee is a dynamic fighter.

edge well tilted, taking off the skin without slicing any meat. Lightly fried and kept as dry of grease as possible, these were sinfully delicious. We tried them later with skin on. The skinless ones are definitely better, but either way they're indescribably excellent.

As anyone in kokanee country already knows, this is a fine fish to smoke. Bringhurst had a smokehouse and his customers kept turning over limits for him to smoke for them before they went home. The flesh is a rich orange. When fresh, kokanee are rather fragile and won't stand lying around in a boat or on a stringer very long. They should be cleaned and refrigerated quickly.

Fortunately, by using Bill Bringhurst's method, you don't have to wait around long anyway. However, after a day or two we discovered, as Bringhurst had predicted, that it was not possible to tell at any given time of day, or on any given day, where the fish would be. They appear to retreat,

230

as he claims, from the sun, going deeper as the surface warms, shifting upward when it cools and darkens toward evening. They also school. Some of the best fishing was always early and late, probably because we used less line then, and thus got more fight and more jumps. I had one good fish on at dusk that leaped six times as fast as it could get from water into the air. It finally went free.

Nowadays the kokanee is being stocked a great deal through the mountain states. And there is a steadily growing interest in it among thousands of anglers in its territory. I recall a few seasons ago, in Utah, when people were puzzling away as to how to catch these fish. The same thing was hap-

I slip them into the ice chest. Kokanee should be handled little and cleaned quickly. They get soft easily.

pening that same year in Wyoming while I was there. Because they are so tricky and erratic, yet awesomely abundant when well started, some places have set snagging seasons on them.

Snagging seasons, where allowed, are set during the spawning run. Like all Western salmons, the kokanee dies after spawning or attempting to spawn. In most waters where it is stocked nowadays, there is little if any opportunity for successful spawning. Thus it is a species easily controlled. Eggs can be taken each spawning season from that crop of adult fish. Fry from those eggs are stocked to replace the lost year-class of spawners, and a stable population thus can be established and perpetuated. Snagging seasons on adult spawn-run fish do no harm because the fish would die anyway. In fact, fish taken at this time are utilized rather than wasted.

The kokanee — also sometimes called blueback, landlocked sockeye, little redfish, silversides and a host of other local names — takes on a riotous red color when on its spawning runs. Natives around West Glacier have told me that McDonald Creek, which runs from McDonald Lake in Glacier National Park out to the Middle Fork of the Flathead River, is literally red when the kokanee run. A snagger attending such a run can hardly miss. Thousands of fish are taken then, chiefly for smoking. Not long ago I noted a news release telling of numerous bald eagles gathered along McDonald Creek, giving snaggers competition.

Each morning when Browning and I now got on Lake Mary Ronan, we used a system of starting with one lure at seven colors, the other at two or three. If neither of us struck silver in a few minutes, we'd work toward each other, one coming up one color, the other dropping one, until we found "the spot." This proved a good procedure for finding them quickly. Sometimes, of course, they just weren't having any,

regardless. Maybe they were elsewhere in the lake. Bringhurst kept insisting that if we'd find the proper depth, and
keep covering the lake, at *some* spot they would always be
willing to "take." Besides, since a good many fishermen were
always on the lake, all we had to do really was sing out:
"How many colors?" Somebody was sure to have 'em
pegged. We decided possibly the fish selected their depth ac-
cording to the depth at which the richest plankton strata lay.

During my stay at Lake Mary Ronan I tried a number of
small lures. We found quite a few they'd hit. A wee
single-hook spoon proved to be hottest of all, in plain silver
or gold, or else with a pink or red head. The ones we used
were very light in weight.

One caution for the first-timer at this method concerns
the lead-core line. When it is let out, you have to thumb the
reel, especially if it's a gear type. Otherwise the line, because
it is heavy, will roll too fast and get into a horrible snarl. I
was reminded, using this line, of the way lead-core was once
used a great deal for deep lake-trout trolling in Ontario. And
this set me thinking about various applications.

I began to surmise that the neat method Bill Bringhurst
had worked out for kokanee might have a very broad use nationally. We know well that schooling bass in the big impoundments, for one example, like to lie at specific depths
and that they desire lures running at exact speeds. White
bass often act the same way. Walleyes are absolutely famous
for their exact-depth, exact-speed requirements. Many saltwater species are, too. Of course, since the fabulous success
of coho and chinook in the Great Lakes, the so-called "down-
rigger" has become very popular as a means for placing lure
or bait at exact depths. This device, attached to boatside,
drops a heavy weight down with the line attached to it. But
when a strike comes, the line is snapped free so the fish can
be played without any inhibiting weight.

However, the down-rigger is a lot of equipment to carry around for kokanee or most freshwater fish. But the "Bring-hurst principle" can be applied easily and economically to all sorts of trolling endeavors. Once you find the proper speed and depth, by following the rules on rod tip and line color, you can reel in a thousand times if need be and still drop right back to the proper position again with no fuss or guess-work.

One thing not to overlook here, however, is the *kind* of lure. Obviously a lure of a specific type and weight will run, at a given number of colors, at a certain depth. When fish are found, the same lure, or its twin, would have to be used in order to put it at the same place again. A lighter or heavier lure would not necessarily run at the same depth. One other little point: A patented rod holder can be used, instead of that nail in the gunwale, to hold the rod in position. And all hands should sit in the middle of the seat. We found, curiously, that in a light skiff, sometimes on calm days too much weight on one side, which raised one tip and lowered the other, made quite a difference in the catch!

Aside from all the possible applications of the method for other species, I am mainly in hopes that this chapter will focus some much-deserved attention upon the little kokanee itself. It is nowadays widely available. It is a species never quite classed, to date, in the big league of game fish. That, as Bill Browning and I, and hordes of Lake Mary Ronan converts, now know, has long been the fault not of the fish but the fisherman. Here is a species that packs a lot of action into one session. While you're catching one trout you can catch ten kokanee—by this method. Once you see one take to the air, you'll know both you and the fish are hooked.

20

You Don't Need
to Carry a Cookbook

Before massive poverty programs required the working class
to split their take with the nonworking class, I was so pleasantly poor that I worked about half as much as I work
today. My wife always told the neighbors that I fished eight
days a week. I tried hard.

During those fine times I had by lunch hour long ago put
aside the typewriter, got my gear together and stuffed it into
my old woods-runner car. About two p.m., after having
anticipated going until it had become an exquisite kind of torture, I'd fix a "lunch" to take along—a handful of crackers
and a paper packet of salt stuffed into my pocket—and be
off.

The places I liked best in those backwoods north-

Michigan days before the population explosion overran them were several far-back, slow brook-trout streams in settings of tamarack and alder bogs where I wallowed almost to my chin. One pool on the Little Pigeon I recall with immense pleasure and a nostalgic gnawing in my gullet.

There was a long, deep run here, and a single tamarack that I progressively decorated with flies. I could never get far enough out into the small river to cast well because of the tree behind me. In my attempts I usually caught two or three barely legal brookies at the wrong end of the hole without ever reaching the good section where I was sure a monster must lie.

The length limit was 7 inches. In those days I could squint at a trout and tell by my hunger if it was long enough. When I had a half-dozen of these I'd get out onto an area of bog solid enough to hold me, break a batch of dry twigs from alders or tamaracks, and start a tiny fire, adding to it while I gutted the trout. A few quick slashes with the knife collected several green willow sticks and whacked the leaves off. Into the mouth of each trout I passed a sharpened stick, ran it on down through the open body cavity and finally thrust it into the tail section. One by one I could now set these sticks slanting into the soft earth so each fish was held only a few inches above the small mound of coals. Five minutes, a turn-over, five minutes more — and the trout were done. Out came the salt and crackers. In the solitude of the swamp I gloried in my feast.

This in my estimation is fish cookery of the classic variety. On a kitchen shelf my wife has a batch of cookbooks, several of which pertain to fish cookery. Some of the recipes are ludicrous. Once I took a bass and did everything to it a certain involved recipe detailed. At the same time I repeated the process with a heavy piece of brown cardboard cut to bass shape. When both were finished, except for the different

236

thickness of the real fish, telling them apart was difficult. One was as tender as the other and both tasted about the same!

I will admit certain sauces do enhance the flavor of fish. But when the condiments or the junk you wallow the catch around in or soak it in or heap on it demolish its texture and overwhelm its natural flavor, then it surely died in vain. Not long ago, for example, I read a lengthy treatise on the preparation of the saltwater sheepshead. The black lining of the body cavity had to be thoroughly scraped away, the thing had to be skinned, the horribly stiff, sharp fins excised, and it was also to be soaked in some vile glop that would soften the big skeletal bones.

The convict-striped saltwater sheepshead is not much of a market fish, nor especially popular as a table fish even with those who like to catch it. Nonetheless, this is one of the most delectable of marine fishes, if prepared in the simplest possible manner. At our house we learned to do this chiefly because we wanted to see what sheepshead *really* tasted like. The fish are gutted, the gills removed. Heads, fins and hide stay put. A broiler pan is greased, a pair of fish are laid on it. Now melted butter is drizzled over each, and you cook 'em until they are done.

From here on, just peel back the tough hide with your fork, lift it off for the cat, shake on salt and pepper. Dig between those big, stiff bones and grub out all the goody. Carefully flip your fish and have at it again. You've never tasted a more delicious fish. It is better than flounder, and flounder is hard to beat.

A great many variations on such simple methods of fish cookery can be concocted by any angler. An old friend of mine used to split a 2-foot chunk of maple log with an ax, then split off a heart piece 2 inches thick to make a rough slab. Each spring he — and sometimes I with him — went into Canada after lake trout. He took the slab along. He'd clean,

Left: Big, delicious brook trout. Split and simply broiled over an open fire, they're superb. *Right:* Saltwater sheepshead. Many anglers don't favor this as a good "eater." Leave the skin on and pan-broil it, peel the skin back, and dig out the white meat from between big bones. Great.

behead, and split open a trout of 4 or 5 pounds, lay it on the plank, drive a few nails along the edge, crisscross copper wire over the fish and secure it to the nails. Then he'd prop that plank before a big heap of hardwood coals that had been forming while he readied the fish and he and compadres assiduously prepared the inner man with red whiskey. The joys of this feast should be confessed with other sins. The art of lurching around a campfire full of trout and bourbon deserves recognition in a college course.

I have long since carried in my tackle a spool of thin wire and a plastic bottle of small brads. On one occasion on the Texas coast a friend and I were miles from any eatery and starving. He had caught a very nice flounder. We walked the beach searching a hunk of driftwood to fit the fish. We found a surf-soaked square of board, affixed the flounder to it by my brads and wire, propped it before a driftwood fire.

238

The red whiskey was missing, but the beer was very cold. I have toyed with the idea of publishing a recipe for "Beered Flounder." Very brief—just pop a cap, glug the suds, and tear into the fish with both hands.

The real fun of fish cookery, for a fisherman, is this on-the-spot business, employing simplicity and ingenuity. Once three of us went walleye fishing, intending to fillet and fry our catch on shore. There is nothing finer than fried walleye fillets, particularly if you use bacon grease in the skillet. I had brought the bacon. Trouble was, nobody caught any walleyes. What we did keep catching, in annoyance, were very fat little largemouth black bass 7 or 8 inches long. By late afternoon these nuisances began to look more and more like supper.

I cut green sticks just as for the small brook trout. The variation was that after I had skewered each small bass through mouth and body cavity on its stick, I wrapped a strip of bacon around it, pinned this in place with whittled slivers. Bass are dry fish, not oily like trout. As the fish sizzled over the coals, the bacon dripped and its flavor permeated them. They were most delicious. I've used the same technique many times since with assortments of small species.

Another variation I've tried several times with large bass, and with other nonoily large fish, is to clean one, cut off the head, split it so it is opened flat. If a plank or board is handy, it can be attached to that. If not, it is secured by the tail to a green stick of at least 1 inch in diameter and propped before the fire, flesh toward the heat. Other short, small, sharpened sticks thrust crosswise into the skin on either side across the back hold the double fillet open. Now a slice or small cut hunk of bacon is skewered high on either side, and in the middle a small peeled onion, pierced here and there with a sharpened stick, is bound to the tail. Onion juice trickles in small amounts as the fish broils. Its aroma rather than any heavy taste permeates the delicious, bacon-flavored flesh.

With my spool of fine wire I have on occasion also made a kind of grill to be hand-held. This is done by bending a long, limber green switch into racquet shape, binding it, then binding on over the racquet area cross pieces of other green switches. An interesting discovery I made with this was in cooking mackerel fresh off the hook. Having run up one of these green-switch grills, I was holding it over a small fire, wondering when my fish would be cooked through. I discovered that limber green sticks of common varieties, if just large enough to support the two sides of a modest-sized mackerel, will be ready to burn in two almost exactly at the time the fish is ready to eat. It's a gambling man's game. Occasionally you have to rake your fish out of the fire!

Rocky coastlines, and the spruce forests of northern lakes or high country, often lack proper green twigs and planking wood. But there will be rocks, and the wherewithal to get a fire going. Also, in these locations the species of fish most likely to be caught will be fairly oily. Find a thin, flat hunk of rock. Get a good bed of coals and lay the rock on top. When it is furiously hot, place a split trout or mackerel on it, skin down. After a bit, take a seashell or sliver of stone and scoop up some glowing embers and ashes. Sprinkle these over the top to sear and brown it. Dust them off when ready to eat, and salt your meal. If ashes bother you, you shouldn't be here!

In a camp where utensils are at hand, methods need not be so primitive, but should still be simple. While frying is the most common, and can turn out utterly delicious results, it is also the setting for more sins against the gullet than any other. Some camp cooks fry fish by laying them in barely warm grease and letting them soak and gently sizzle until they disintegrate into a pastiness that might be termed the "Gall Bladder Special." Others literally boil them in oil.

Frying fish is so basic that its virtue should not end in butchery. Actually, a light dusting of flour beats corn meal because there is less taste to it. Then a quick treatment in a hot skillet with as little grease as possible, and using fish as small as possible, completes the deal. But a friend of mine devised an interesting method for just tasting the fish and nothing else. An avid fly-fisherman for bluegills, he removed head, fins, tail. These neat-looking triangles he wiped dry, greased lightly, laid in a Teflon skillet. Gentle frying browned them, yet there was no flour or other crust. Though I did not believe it would work, they were wonderful.

A simple wire grill is the handiest camp utensil for preparing all kinds of fish, because it allows easy broiling when laid across rocks or logs. For a rush job with small fish, I used to carry in the trunk of my car a coffee can with top and bottom removed. This ring I thrust into coals. Over it I placed a small wire grill. The idea was to concentrate the heat, keep it all going straight up. Panfish or small pompano and spadefish I have fixed this way on the beach have been superb.

In Europe fish stock—made from boiling heads, fins, skeletons and odds and ends of fish, then straining off the liquor—has always been indispensable, yet it is almost never heard of in this country. This stock is used to baste or moisten a large baked fish, or as the basic ingredient in all sorts of sauces. Perhaps it has never occurred to anglers who keep grumbling when small panfish gobble bait or hit lures, either in fresh or salt water, that they are throwing back a most important element of many an elegant camp dish.

For instance, on one occasion I kept, over the protests of my companions, several dozen small sunfishes. We were bug-fishing for bass. These small fish kept somehow getting attached to the big poppers. I cleaned and beheaded the lot of them. I knew my camp companions would gag at the thought if I merely gutted them and then boiled them heads

On a back-bush trip in Ontario, guide cooks lake trout fillets the quick way while we wait, mouths watering.

Too many fancy recipes ruin fresh fish. Simple procedures outdoors or in are best. A fine way to fix a flounder is to skewer it to a driftwood board and broil it before a beach fire. A snapper can just be lightly oiled and go onto the grill.

and all. When I had a large heap of them ready, I put them into a kettle with enough water to cover them. Now I placed them over the coals and got them bubbling gently, after which I raked away some coals so they merely simmered.

There they stayed for an hour. At this time salt and pepper went in, plus several onion slices, and some celery tops I cut from a bunch found in the cooler. Other items might have been added — carrot, parsley. None was available. When this had cooked another half-hour I skimmed it, strained it through a clean dish towel. This liquor was then

242

set aside to cool and finally placed in a container in the ice chest.

With this stock as a starter point, it is surprising how many excellent dishes can be prepared. In fact, the stock itself, thickened a wee bit with flour, and with boiled potatoes or plain butter beans added and served steaming, is a solid and delectable meal. As a start for chowder, or to heat and pour with melted butter over a baked fish, such stock is wonderful. The same thing can be done, obviously, with small saltwater species. I pitched a batch of diminutive bait-stealing croakers into a bucket one time, cleaned them and made a similar stock from them, then used it as the base for a chowder made from big boneless hunks of a huge drum too tough and ancient to eat otherwise. It was the talk for the rest of the trip around the beach cottage where we were staying.

But about those sunfishes. . . . One lucky gent tied into a bass of 8 pounds. We cleaned it and made a stuffing for it—about 1¹/₂ cups of crumbled-up bread, some chopped onion lightly browned in butter, salt, pepper, an egg beaten up and mixed in to hold the stuffing together, and the melted butter from cooking the onion tossed in. We sewed the fish up after stuffing by trussing it with a hunk of woven backing line. We had no roaster. So, we curled the big bass up in an iron kettle, greased beforehand. We then heated a cup of that rich stock and poured it in. With the cover on, the kettle went onto the coals.

Admittedly, nobody really knew what would happen. It was comical to see everyone standing around listening, sniffing, every now and then peeking into the pot. When it looked dry, in went a bit more stock. Then one gent thought of some wine he'd brought, and gave it a slop over the baking bass, as basting material. We got to passing the wine around. First thing you know, the bass is baked . . . or half-boiled . . . cooked, anyway. We heated up some of the remaining stock and served it spooned over the stuffing from the bass. The same gent who had found the wine just happened to locate another bottle. It was red. You want to bet red wine won't go with fish? The meal was memorable.

Here are two more to try in camp. The first one I tried originally with a 9-pound pike. Obviously, other fish will do just as well. Many anglers spurn pike. A big one eats superbly. Fillet the fish and skin the fillets. Make some stuffing—bread crumbs, diced onion and celery, some melted butter, salt, pepper, a pinch of sage, a drizzle of lemon juice if it's handy.

Grease a Dutch oven and lay in one fillet. Pile on and smooth stuffing, lay on another fillet, dribble on a bit of butter, plus salt and pepper. At home you could cover and bake this at around 350 degrees for half an hour, then uncover and brown the top. In camp, guess at it. Don't get it too darned hot. To brown the top over a campfire, uncover, lay a grill across, gently place a few large coals on the grill for a few minutes.

The second item: fish cakes to vary the camp routine. Skin some fillets. Boil them gently in a small amount of water. When done, flake each and be sure all bones are removed. Use equal parts of these fish flakes and mashed potato. The packaged kind works fine. Mix together, with one egg added for each cup of the mixture, plus chopped onion, salt, pepper. Make this into patties, dust on a little flour, and fry quickly so not to soak with grease. Great for breakfast!

As important as cooking fish, it seems to me, is a willingness to *try* various fishes. Just because somebody says it isn't a good eating fish isn't a reason for turning it down. When I first came to Texas everybody looked at me as if I was cracked when I asked why they threw away or gave away Spanish mackerel and kingfish. Yet *they* relished gaff-top catfish, a good enough saltwater fish but nothing to compare with kingfish steak or broiled mackerel.

Fish get known as "not fitten" for a variety of reasons, most of them ridiculous. As a kid, I ate bullheads by the peck. My grandmother knew how to slip the skeletons out and lay them flat in a crock, a layer of salt, a layer of bullheads, placed in the cool cellarway. We didn't have a refrigerator, and in those days no ice man cameth. In Texas where I now live people call bullheads "pollywogs" and would as soon eat a cannibal as clean one. For fun I filleted a whole batch of "pollywogs," shook 'em in flour, deep-fried 'em the way any Tejano would cook his catfish. We fed them to cat-lovin' friends, and lo, did they lick 'em up!

Another facet of fish fixing never to be overlooked is smoking. It is not an easy art. A really good permanent smokehouse is a fairly complicated structure. Nonetheless, you can do pretty well with a spike-camp rig.

I laugh aloud at my first attempt, even though it turned out darned good. I'd been told to make a brine that would float an egg, soak the cleaned fish (heads on, gills out) in it overnight, hang 'em on a line to drip dry. My instruction from here on was to make a smokehouse of two big wooden packing boxes. One was to be upset, open top down, over a trench. Holes were bored in the top at one side. Over the holes was set, upended, the other box, a somewhat smaller one. Inside this one wires were run across and the fish, split open, were to be laid on these. A fire was built in the trench; up went the smoke through the boxes.

Actually, this outfit works fine. You must use hard woods such as maple or hickory, never any pitch woods. In the Southwest mesquite is wonderful. The fire must burn slowly, smokily, with plenty of attention. To smoke fish you do not want *heat*—just warm smoke, hour after hour. You *cure,* not cook them. It can take two or three days.

However, I didn't have any boxes. I did have a wooden barrel. I knocked the bottom out. I didn't have any proper wood. Besides, I was in a hurry, which no fish smoker ever should be. I did have some green-dry alfalfa hay. Don't laugh yet. I made a fire of hay in the bottomless barrel. I draped strings of small fish across the top on wires, and clapped the cover on. Over and over. I think they partly cooked. But let me tell you — although tough from their brine bath, they were really delicious, and they kept for weeks. A few beers and a box of those home-smoked, salty, rubber-tough fish make a hit with all the neighbors.

Once on a high-country trout trip two of us tried smoking fish an old Indian and frontier way. We dug a fire pit in the ground and got a good bunch of coals going. Over it we made a tepee out of fresh-cut aspen poles. Now we took a couple of tarps used as pannier covers on the pack animals and draped these around the poles with the top left open as a flue. We hung strings of one-pound cleaned trout, previously salted for a night and then wiped dry, pole to pole inside near the apex. We fed the coals with axed chips of whatever non-coniferous woods we could find. At night the smoke would die. Next morning we'd build a big fire outside, shovel coals into our pit and start fresh. Taking turns, we alternately fished and tended the smokehouse. In three days we had a beautiful batch of trout to carry with us the remainder of the pack trip for lunches and in-betweens.

Building a really efficient smokehouse at home can be fun. Or, today you can buy contraptions for smoking fish all ready-made. It's a good hobby. So is all kinds of fish cookery. But the item of prime importance is to make up your own methods and dishes. Don't carry a cookbook. How do you suppose the guy who says "use two cups" found out that was the proper amount? Hell, he used one, or three, and ruined his supper!